NATIONALISM AND COMMUNISM
IN CHILE

Center for International Studies
Massachusetts Institute of Technology

Studies in Communism, Revisionism, and Revolution
(formerly *Studies in International Communism*)
William E. Griffith, general editor

Nationalism and Communism in Chile ★

ERNST HALPERIN

THE M.I.T. PRESS
MASSACHUSETTS INSTITUTE OF TECHNOLOGY
CAMBRIDGE, MASSACHUSETTS

Second Printing, December 1970

ISBN 2 262 08020 6 (hardcover)

Library of Congress Catalog Card Number: 65-21569

Printed in the United States of America

PREFACE

Although some monographs on the history of individual communist parties have been published, the study of the current policies of these parties, particularly of those not in power, is a neglected field. Yet such studies are of value to statesmen and scholars alike. The communist parties are members of a movement that until very recently was under rigid discipline and centralized leadership. Events at the Moscow center — power struggles, conflicts of opinion, drastic policy changes — were faithfully and rapidly reflected in the policies of even the smallest and least important communist parties, sometimes months or even years before the event itself became known to the noncommunist world. A pronouncement by the Communist Party of Norway, Switzerland, or Martinique might be utterly irrelevant to the Norwegian, Swiss, or Martiniquaise political situation, but it might well contain some hidden phrase highly relevant to the situation prevailing in Moscow. Today, when the international communist movement is reeling under the impact of the Sino-Soviet conflict, and central authority and discipline are fast disintegrating, careful observation of the policies and analysis of the statements of its member parties are as important as ever.

One major obstacle that has hitherto impeded the utilization of this important source of information is the obscurity of communist terminology. To those not in possession of highly specialized knowledge, the typical communist document appears to be a hodgepodge of wild vituperation against the imperialists, totally unrealistic descriptions of the state of the country and of the world, fervent praise of the people's masses, who are alleged to be rallying to the party's banner in ever greater numbers, and of self-criticism of the party for not having made full use of its opportunities and for having been either too sanguine or too pessimistic in its assessment of the situation. The one message that appears to come through clearly in all these documents is that of the party's devotion to the cause of revolution. But hidden under this revolutionary verbiage, communist party pronouncements usually contain far more.

In order to understand communist party documents one must first of all realize that they are not meant for the man in the street, whom the party prefers to woo with brief and unsophisticated slogans. The long, immensely involved, and tediously repetitive policy statements are intended to explain the party's current policy to the cadres while at the same time strengthening the cadres' faith — a secular creed that may be summed up in the words "Salvation through Revolution." That is why the explanation of the party's policy, and the announcement of any changes therein, are always obscured by voluble assurances that the revolution is inevitable, and not too far away, and that the party's current policy, be it leftist or rightist, extremist or moderate, violent or peaceful, isolationist or collaborationist, is the only effectively revolutionary one. The untrained reader almost invariably mistakes this revolutionary verbiage for the message of the document.

"Nothing has changed" was the noncommunist world's comment on the Seventh Congress of the Comintern in 1935. The momentous decision to switch from a policy of hostility toward the democratic parties of the left and center to one of collaboration with them — a decision that was soon profoundly to affect the destinies of Spain and, to a lesser degree, of France — was overlooked, while the accompanying declarations of loyalty to the principle of world revolution were regarded as the essential result of the congress.

In the same way, the noncommunist world has often missed the significance of changes in the leadership of individual communist parties, regarding them as the result of petty squabbles between men who were agreed on the basic points of doctrine, whereas these changes were actually often a reflection of important policy decisions by the rulers of the Soviet Union. One instance of this was the downfall of the American Communist Party chief Earl Browder in 1945. Browder's entire policy had been based on the assumption that Soviet-American wartime cooperation, and consequently also the extremely moderate wartime policies of the Western communist parties, would continue in the postwar period. The first attack on Browder — by the French Communist Jacques Duclos — was launched as early as April 1945, before the war in Europe had come to a close. This attack, and Browder's subsequent removal from office, caused a sensation throughout the international communist movement, being correctly interpreted as the first result of a basic decision in Moscow that Soviet postwar policy toward the United States would be one of antagonism and not of cooperation. If the special knowledge needed in order to arrive at such a correct interpretation of what seemingly appeared to be a minor crisis in an unimportant political group had been available to, and given credence by, Western statesmen, they would have been able to adjust to the harsh reality of Soviet postwar policy much earlier. The world would have been spared years of fumbling and also the recriminations of those who maintain that a benevolent Soviet government was reluctantly pushed into a position of hostility by the postwar blunders of the West.

Later, unfamiliarity with communist terminology caused Western statesmen to misinterpret the Sino-Soviet conflict and to underestimate its importance. For years they insisted that this was a mere quarrel about tactics, and that Peking and Moscow were united in their basic aim: the destruction of capitalism. The further course of events has, however, made it abundantly clear that the basic unity of principle suggested by a superficial reading of communist documents is a myth. Meanwhile, the number of those who have learned how to translate the complicated terminology of these documents into the crude language of power politics is increasing, and the interest of political scientists in the international communist movement and its member parties has been stimulated by the fact that the movement has become one of the main battle-grounds of the Sino-Soviet conflict.

This study of communism and nationalism in Chile was carried out in the framework of a survey of the communist movement, with special reference to the Sino-Soviet conflict, under the direction of William E. Griffith and under the auspices of the Center for International Studies, Massachusetts Institute of Technology. In order to give a picture of the specific conditions in which the Chilean Communists operate, it was found necessary to include chapters on their main ally, the Socialist Party, and their most effective opponent, the Christian Democrats — two groups representative of the extreme nationalist and the moderate nationalist currents that are the most dynamic political forces in Latin America today.

The Center for International Studies, Massachusetts Institute of Technology, and its Director, Max F. Millikan, have made it possible for me to write this book and to conduct extensive research in Chile in 1963 and 1964. I am deeply grateful to William E. Griffith for his confidence in me and for his tireless encouragement. The arduous task of preparing the manuscript for publication was undertaken by the Center's editors, Richard W. Hatch and Jean P. S. Clark. The quotations were checked by Robin A. Remington, the index prepared by Peter R. Prifti, and the typing done by Lila T. Rose. The responsibility for all errors and omissions, as well as for the views and opinions expressed in this book, is mine.

Ernst Halperin

Rio de Janeiro
April 1965

CONTENTS

NATIONALISM AND COMMUNISM
IN CHILE

I

NATIONALISM AND COMMUNISM IN LATIN AMERICA

NATIONALISM

The economic and political hegemony of the United States over Latin America appears to be a natural consequence of the region's geographical position. Yet this belief, so widely held among Latin Americans, is erroneous. Domination and subjection are political and economic, not geographical, categories. And whereas the geographical position of a region is immutable, the political and economic conditions prevailing within it are subject to change.

Latin America was not always the "back yard of the United States." There were once great and highly civilized empires in the area, while the area that is today the United States was a wilderness roamed by nomad tribes. Those empires were crushed by invaders from another continent, other invaders penetrated the wilderness, and for centuries both areas were under European domination. Spain, Portugal, Britain, France, and the Netherlands established their colonies in the Western Hemisphere, and smaller European powers also made their presence felt. Even the Kurlanders, whose land is now a part of the Soviet Union, were at one time active in the Caribbean.

Dissensions among the European powers finally enabled both the Anglo-Saxons of the north and the Latins of the south to shake off European tutelage. At that time, and for several decades afterward, a number of Latin American states were still economically stronger and in some respects culturally more advanced than the United States. As the United States grew stronger, it encroached on the territory of its neighbor Mexico and then advanced farther south. Yet these typically imperialistic activities, which comprised both economic penetration and military aggression, were confined to Mexico and Central America, and for all their violence, they led neither to the complete domination of that area nor to the total elimination of European competitors. To this day Britain, France, and the Netherlands continue to hold positions in the Caribbean.

North American economic penetration of the South American continent was a very much slower process and was not accompanied by territorial encroachment and military aggression. Throughout the nineteenth and well into the twentieth century the dominant economic power and most important outside political influence in most of South America was not the United States but Britain. Even in the period between the two world wars British economic power was still so strong in South America that the Soviet Communists assumed this region to be one of the main battlefields in a

British-American struggle for domination of the capitalist world, a struggle that according to both Trotsky and Stalin would inevitably lead to a war between these two powers.

The economic competition of Britain and the United States was of course not the life-and-death struggle that the Soviet Marxists assumed it to be. Indeed, it might have continued indefinitely if Britain had not been seriously weakened and forced to retrench by its second armed conflict with Germany, World War II.

The United States thus did not actively push its British competitor out of South America; it was left in economic control of the region by default. Only at this point, at the end of World War II, did all of Latin America really become "the back yard of the United States," even though the term may have been coined earlier.

United States economic hegemony over South America thus is a very recent phenomenon. It is precisely because it is so new and unfamiliar that it has given rise to a wave of anti-Americanism far more violent than that of the Mexicans, who in the past suffered much more from "Yankee imperialism" but who have had time to become accustomed to the overpowering presence of their northern neighbor. In their state of traumatic shock, many South Americans have even lost consciousness of the fact that United States hegemony over their region is new, that the United States at one time played a very different role on their continent — that of an ally against attempts at domination by European powers.

Three different basic attitudes toward the hard fact of United States hegemony may be observed among politically conscious Latin Americans. First, there is the attitude called *entreguismo,* that is, surrender. It actually comprises a whole gamut of attitudes and opinions, ranging from the belief that what is good for the United States is also good for Latin America to the mere acceptance of United States hegemony as an inevitability that must be faced and lived with. Yet wholehearted espousal of American political doctrines and of the American way of life is not very common among the *entreguistas,* many of whom compensate for their acceptance of North American economic and military superiority by stressing the superiority of European culture. But all *entreguistas* agree in advocating unrestricted North American private investment in their countries and unconditional support of United States foreign policy by their governments.

In opposition to this attitude of surrender and acceptance, a broad sector of Latin American public opinion believes in the need for self-assertion. The partisans of this "assertive nationalism" hold that foreign companies should either be nationalized or at least be forced to contribute their maximum to the economic development of the country in which they are operating. In foreign policy they are in favor of demonstrations of independence. They reject the view that unconditional support of the United States in the international sphere is necessary in order to ensure good relations with that country. On the other hand the "assertive nationalists" concede that the United States, in view of its overwhelming material superiority, has a special role to play in the hemisphere. They are not basically anti-American. Respect and even enthusiasm for North American political philosophies and cultural achievements are more widespread among them than among the politically and economically subservient *entreguistas.*

The third attitude is one of total rebellion or "strategic hatred," as Eduardo Frei terms it.[1] The extreme nationalists who adopt this attitude are not willing, like the merely "assertive nationalists," to negotiate better terms with the United States. They will not be satisfied by anything less than the complete withdrawal of the United States from Latin America. They are not against any specific United States policy but against all United States policies, because their obsessive anti-Yankeeism is not caused by mere mistakes in United States policy. It is the result of pride wounded by the very existence of United States superiority, the mere presence of the United States in Latin America, regardless of the forms in which this presence manifests itself. They can be satisfied only by the destruction of United States power. They are proud men who do not want to live in a rich man's back yard and have come to the conclusion that the only way to free themselves from their back-yard status is to burn down the big house in front.

Since the combined might of the Latin American states would not suffice to overcome the United States, the extreme nationalists look for the aid of an outside power capable of challenging the United States, a policy of seeking the support of one big power against another that has been followed by the weak throughout

[1] See Eduardo Frei M., *Pensamiento y acción* (Santiago de Chile: Editorial Del Pacífico, 1956), pp. 227 f. Frei distinguishes among the three attitudes of *entreguismo,* "constructive cooperation," and "strategic hatred." Robert J. Alexander, in his *Today's Latin America* (New York: Doubleday, 1962) and elsewhere, terms the proponents of extreme nationalism or "strategic hatred" the "Jacobin Left."

the course of history. But in our times power politics take on the form of ideological strife, one result of which is that the real issues, which in this case are the relations between Latin American states and the United States and the attempts of extrahemispheric powers to set foot in the Western Hemisphere, are obscured both to the onlooker and to some extent even to the participants themselves. Thus in the 1930's and during the Second World War Latin American extreme nationalism sought the aid of Germany and Italy against both Britain and the United States. In the process the extreme nationalists adopted the language and the organizational forms of European fascism. After the destruction of fascism in the Second World War, the Latin American extreme nationalists sought and found a new ally against the United States: the Soviet Union. They therefore began to talk the language of Marxism-Leninism.

Besides being the only power capable of defying the United States, the Soviet Union also stands for a program of complete social and economic transformation that makes it even more attractive to many Latin Americans. The desire for social change is widespread in Latin America. Since such change would of course also affect the American-owned enterprises that play such an important role in the economy of most Latin American countries, and since the United States government has frequently declared its determination to protect the interests of American investors abroad, the United States itself seems to Latin Americans to be one of the major obstacles to the social change that they desire.[2]

[2] To many Latin Americans there appears to be an inherent contradiction in the Alliance for Progress, which advocates both social

Nationalistic resentment of United States hegemony over Latin America and the Latin Americans' desire for social change, to which the United States appears to constitute an obstacle, have thus blended in the postwar period to produce a powerful upsurge of pro-Soviet and anti-American sentiment.

For the first decade of the postwar era the possibility of the Soviet Union's exerting any strong influence in Latin America was still severely limited by the fact that the Western Hemisphere was out of range of Soviet military power. This situation was drastically changed in 1957 when the Soviet Union put an intercontinental ballistic missile into operation. That scientific achievement, which has brought about what may well be termed the greatest revolution of military strategy in the history of mankind, made it possible for a Eurasian power situated literally on the other side of the globe directly to threaten the Western Hemisphere with destruction. The Soviet Union was now in a position to employ nuclear blackmail to protect a base established in Latin America.

Some three years after this possibility had emerged, the Soviet Union did in fact establish a base for political and military operations in the Western Hemisphere. It is significant that it did not obtain the base through the offices of a Latin American communist party, none of which were in a position to seize power, but through alliance with a Latin American nationalist.

---

reform and an increase in private investment. Latin Americans argue that those governments determined to implement effective social reforms are not the ones likely to inspire confidence in the domestic and foreign private investor. Actually the contradiction is more apparent than real. The example of Venezuela shows that reform governments easily win the investor's confidence once they have demonstrated a certain stability.

It is doubtful that Fidel Castro contemplated a complete break with the United States and the inclusion of Cuba in the "socialist camp" when he first took up the Soviet offer to back him in 1959. At that time he may well have contemplated nothing more than a balancing act between the two powers. The United States government did not intend to tolerate the existence of a pocket Nasser in the Caribbean, but its countermeasures were worse than self-defeating. It committed exactly the same mistake that John Foster Dulles made in Egypt in 1956, and the results were even more negative. Instead of warning the Soviets that it would on no account permit their expansion into the area, the United States applied pressure on the small state seeking Soviet aid. By thus giving the impression of being afraid to face the Soviets, it encouraged Castro to draw ever closer to his new Soviet protector.

The failure of the United States to prevent Soviet economic and military assistance to Castro and its unwillingness to face up to the real threat to its interests in Latin America, which was the Soviet Union and not little Cuba, had a galvanizing effect on Latin American nationalism. Here was what the extreme nationalists had been waiting for: the chance with the help of a great foreign power to free their countries from United States domination. They were all too ready to interpret the apparent weakness of the United States as confirmation of the Soviet claim that the world balance of power had shifted decisively in favor of the "socialist camp." Marxism-Leninism became the ideological cloak of Latin American extreme nationalism, as fascism had been its cloak in a previous period.

With the Cubans leading the way, from 1960 onward

Castroite movements sprang up in every Latin American country either as independent groups or as Castroite wings in the left-of-center mass parties. The most prominent among these movements were the Movimiento de Izquierda Revolucionaria (MIR) and the left wing of the moderate URD (Unión Republicana Democrática) party in Venezuela, the Movimiento Obrero Estudiantil Campesino (MOEC) and a sector of the Liberal Party in Colombia, the APRA (Alianza Popular Revolucionaria Americana) *Rebelde* (later MIR) in Peru, Julião's Peasant Leagues in Brazil, the left wing of the Peronistas in Argentina, and a strong pro-Castroite trend in the Socialist Party of Chile.

The ideology of all these groups was Marxist-Leninist, and they all stood for revolution and the installation of a socialist regime on the Cuban pattern in their own country. To the nonspecialist they were indistinguishable from communist party-liners. They all seemed to be part of a vast conspiracy centered in Moscow, Prague, Peking, and Havana. Yet there were some vitally important differences between these groups and the communist parties of Latin America.

First, unlike the communist parties all have maintained an independent attitude toward the Sino-Soviet conflict. Although only the Soviet Union (and not China) is in a position to give them effective support in the struggle against the United States, none has taken the Soviet side and come out in condemnation of the Chinese. Their reason is that they cannot accept the Soviet formula of Peaceful Coexistence, which implies at least the possibility of a long-term accommodation with the United States. They are pro-Soviet only as long as the Soviet Union conducts an all-out relentless struggle against the United States. In other words, they are moved by what they consider to be the interests of their own countries, whereas the communists are willing to subordinate these interests to those of world revolution as represented by the Soviet Union.

Second, the Marxism-Leninism professed by these groups is only skin deep, and it is not of the Soviet brand. Their indoctrination is not nearly as thorough as that of the communist party cadres. In most groups what is called "Marxism-Leninism" boils down to acceptance of the Marxist doctrine of "exploitation of man by man" and of the Leninist doctrine of imperialism as the last stage of capitalism. In practice if not in theory all of them reject the Soviet formula of the Peaceful Road to socialism. And many of them prefer "Che" Guevara's thesis that in Latin America the peasantry is a more important and more effective revolutionary force than the Marxist-Leninist doctrine of the proletariat as the "main force of the revolution."

On all these points the Castroite groups of extreme nationalists differ profoundly from the great majority of the Latin American communist parties.

COMMUNISM

The noncommunist and dissident communist groups of the Latin American Left are unanimous in accusing the communist parties of not being genuinely revolutionary. Remembering the French saying, *On est toujours le réactionnaire de quelqu'un,* one is inclined to dismiss this accusation as stemming from mere envy or blind fanaticism. Every communist party in the world, even the most successful, has at one time or another been denounced by rivals and competitors as having betrayed the revolution, or at least as lacking all revolutionary fervor. Even Lenin himself was once accused by the Mensheviks of Bernsteinian revisionism.

Yet it is an error to apply European or Asian standards to Latin American reality. In other parts of the world it may be merely ridiculous to claim that the communists are not revolutionaries, but in Latin America it is a fact that the communist movement has no vigorous revolutionary tradition. There is probably no conservative or liberal party in all of Latin America that has not staged more insurrections and incited more civil wars than the communists. In a continent racked by civil strife the communists' record has been one of remarkable quiescence. Their one major attempt to seize power by force was the 1935 insurrection led by Luiz Carlos Prestes in Brazil, apart from which there have been only some instances of communist participation in risings organized by noncommunist groups.[3] Of late, communist party leaders in Latin America have been under strong pressure from Castroite elements to switch over to a policy of terrorism and guerrilla warfare, but so far only the Venezuelan communists have succumbed to this pressure and changed their party line.

Their lack of revolutionary fervor does not mean that the communist parties of Latin America are democratic. They are totalitarian parties with a totalitarian system of organization and a totalitarian mentality, and whenever they have managed to maneuver themselves into a position where they enjoy at least a share of real

[3] The peasant rising of January 1932 in the Central American republic of El Salvador was sparked off, but not actually led, by the Communists, whose leaders were jailed before the rising began.

power, as in Chile for a few months during 1946 and 1947, in Guatemala in 1954, in Cuba from 1960 onward, their totalitarianism has at once become manifest in their behavior toward both allies and opponents.

One vital element of totalitarianism, however, is missing: the drive, the ruthless determination to seize power at all costs. In general the communist parties of Latin America do not strive very hard for power. They are content to play the normal game of Latin American politics, cooperating both with dictators and with democrats in return for small benefits. This is understandable in view of the fact that until a short time ago a communist regime in Latin America could not have expected effective Soviet protection against intervention by the dominant power of the hemisphere — the United States.

Communism first made its appearance in Latin America in the early 1920's, at a time when it was possible to believe that the revolution in Russia was the immediate prelude to revolution on a world scale. This assumption proved false. World revolution did not materialize, and the Soviet Union remained isolated, weak, racked by internal dissension, and more and more absorbed by its gigantic effort of industrialization. It could not have come to the assistance of a revolution in any Latin American country.

In consequence the ultraleftist strategy of immediate revolution — the so-called "third period" strategy — which was launched by the Communist International in 1929, made even less sense in Latin America than in Europe. All the strikes and petty revolts engineered by the Latin American communists in obedience to the orders of the Comintern failed miserably, and the one serious attempt made by a communist party to seize power by violence, the Prestes revolt in Brazil in 1935, was also a failure. The communist parties of Latin America — not very strong from the beginning — lost all influence and dwindled into insignificance.

But at the very moment of the Brazilian rising another communist party, that of Chile, was already preparing to implement the Popular Front strategy newly proclaimed by the Comintern. This new strategy, calling for broad alliances with limited aims, was soon adopted by all the communist parties of the hemisphere.

From the moment of the adoption of the Popular Front strategy the history of the Latin American communist parties has been one of the most extraordinary opportunism. Communist parties have indiscriminately cooperated with dictators and with democratic parties of the Right as well as the Left. Sometimes they have split into two parties with opposing policies, one collaborating with a dictator and the other with the democratic opposition, only to reunite after the political situation had changed.[4]

The communist parties of Latin America were thus allowed almost complete freedom of maneuver by the leadership of the international communist movement, while the communist parties of Europe (and that of the United States) were kept on a short leash and obliged to respond to the slightest change in Soviet foreign policy. The reason why the Latin American

---

[4] For a detailed account of the somewhat sordid history of the communist parties of Latin America, see Robert J. Alexander, *Communism in Latin America* (2nd printing; New Brunswick, N.J.: Rutgers University Press, 1960). Rollie E. Poppino's *International Communism in Latin America* (New York: Free Press of Glencoe, 1964), deals with the same subject in a more summary fashion and includes an assessment of communism's possibilities in the area.

communists were accorded such freedom of movement was undoubtedly that throughout the 1930's and 1940's, and during most of the 1950's, Soviet foreign policy had far more pressing concerns than Latin America. The area was beyond the pale of Soviet state interest not only because it was out of reach of the Soviet armed forces but also because none of the Latin American countries carried enough weight in international affairs for the Soviets to be vitally concerned about their friendship or enmity. Consequently the activities of the Latin American communists were only rarely considered to be of importance to the Soviet Union. They were not expected to seize power or to maintain themselves in power if by some fluke they managed to seize it.

Their freedom of maneuver has caused the Latin American communists to be drawn into the normal game of political give-and-take to a far greater extent than the communist parties in other parts of the world. Even in those Latin American countries where they are clandestine the communist parties are a factor taken into account both by the government and by the opposition in their everyday political dealings. It is true that most of these parties are very small, but that only makes it easier and less dangerous to cooperate with them. The few thousand votes controlled by a communist party may swing an election; its influence among university students may serve to start or quell a riot; its trade-union connections may be of use to a military dictator struggling to improve his image and win a civilian following. And since the Latin American communists' principles are very flexible their support may be bought, and at a moderate price — perhaps by an amnesty for their imprisoned comrades and a slight relaxation of police supervision, or by the offer of a few positions in the state-controlled trade-union bureaucracy, or by the permission to operate a daily newspaper or even a mere magazine.

Visiting Europeans and North Americans are frequently appalled by the average Latin American politico's readiness to negotiate and conclude deals with the local communist party. In their experience this is the road to perdition: Those who collaborate with the communist party inevitably become the party's prisoners. But that is not the case in Latin America, where politicians who wish to shake off their communist allies when these have exhausted their usefulness have rarely found it difficult to do so. With the possible exception of Chile, the communist parties of the Latin American countries are simply too weak to constitute a serious danger to their allies.

The weakness and inefficacy of Latin American communism stem from the fact that the organizational principles and techniques of world communism are not effective in the specific conditions of Latin America. The organizational formula of the communist world movement, Democratic Centralism, is extreme centralization and rigid discipline. But abstract loyalty to an organization representing principle is poorly developed in Latin America. Perhaps because the traditions of feudalism are still strong throughout the region, the average Latin American prefers to give his loyalty to an individual or to a family. In consequence "organization men" are scarce in Latin America, and political parties based on ideologies, as well as trade unions, cooperatives, and similar organizations, are more difficult to build up and tend to be far less efficient than in Europe.

Furthermore the Latin American communists have been led by their Marxist credo to concentrate their organizational efforts on the industrial workers and especially on those groups already organized in trade unions. Unfortunately for them, these groups usually constitute a privileged stratum of the Latin American proletariat, a "workers' aristocracy" as Lenin called it, and are not really a revolutionary element at all.

To put it briefly, the Marxist-Leninist concept of revolution by the organized working class is not applicable to Latin America, first, because the Latin American working class as a whole can hardly be organized; second, because those sectors that can be organized are not revolutionary.[5]

For these reasons in the view of the communists, conditions in Latin America are never quite ripe for revolution — because revolution has to be made by "the masses," and "the masses" have to be prepared for revolution by a very long and patient labor of organization and propaganda that is never quite completed.[6]

[5] There are of course some exceptions to this rule. Thus the well-organized Bolivian tin miners took a decisive part in the Bolivian revolution. It is, however, significant that these miners were not organized by the communists but by a typical leftist-nationalist Latin American caudillo, Juan Lechín.

[6] Thus, for instance, the Peruvian Communist Jorge del Prado, in an article characteristically entitled "Everything with the Masses, Nothing Without Them," states:

International experience — including that of the Cuban revolution with all its promises — as well as our own still recent experience confirm the Peruvian communists in their conviction that the Marxist-Leninist postulates that the masses make the revolution and that there cannot be revolution without the support of the masses are still valid. . . . Confronting these postulates with the possibilities of the actual situation in our country, we come to the conclusion that even though there are clear symptoms that the majority of the Peruvian people feel the need for radical changes in the general conditions of life, and although it is also

Latin American communist parties have often continued to repeat this argument against immediate action right up to the moment that some other group actually has to make the revolution, usually in some highly unorthodox and typically Latin American manner.

The need for long and patient work of organization and propaganda is also used by the Latin American communists — and probably in perfectly good faith — to justify their many unprincipled pacts with dictators. Since organization and propaganda are rendered extremely difficult if the party is obliged to operate in complete clandestinity, with its newspapers suppressed, its leaders imprisoned, and its trade-union organizers eliminated, it becomes the duty of the party leadership to obtain and safeguard the privileges of legality even at the cost of a morally dubious compromise with a dictator. In this manner the very dictum that the masses must be organized for revolution has served as an excuse for the shadiest deals with dictators such as Trujillo of Santo Domingo, Somoza of Nicaragua, and Batista of Cuba. Thus most of the communist parties of Latin America have degenerated into machines run by professional politicians who hire out their services to dictators and democrats alike in return for petty concessions.

---

true that today there is a vigorous pressure of vast sectors in favor of these changes, this process has not yet resulted in (and cannot of itself result in) inculcating in the masses the conviction that the fundamental problem is that of undertaking the conquest of political power.

(Translation from *Nuestra Epoca* [the Chilean edition of *Problems of Peace and Socialism*], No. 5, 1964, p. 13. In this and similar quotations I have used my own translation of the more complete Spanish text instead of the English version published in the *World Marxist Review*, which is frequently condensed.)

NATIONALISTS AND COMMUNISTS

The one-time communist revolutionaries who had degenerated into machine politicians were unable to take full advantage of the wave of pro-Soviet feeling that swept Latin America in the 1950's and early 1960's. The bulk of the nationalists who had become admirers of the Soviet Union stayed outside the party, and the Castroite groups they formed soon came into conflict with the party-line communists. The intensity of the conflict, which in some parties became evident as early as 1960, has greatly increased since the Cuban crisis of 1962. In two Latin American countries the Castroite nationalists have gained the upper hand over the communists. In Cuba Fidel Castro himself is in undisputed command of the new Marxist-Leninist "United Party of the Socialist Revolution" (PURS — Partido Unido de la Revolución Socialista) and has relegated the old-guard communists to positions of secondary importance. In Venezuela Castroite nationalists have gained control of the Communist Party itself and caused it to depart from its traditional loyalty to Moscow. In other countries there is open strife between the communists and the Castroites, and in those countries where a formal alliance is still maintained, relations between the two groups are very strained.

The issue at stake in this conflict is a highly practical one: the timing and strategy of the revolution. The Castroite groups want their revolution now; the communists say that conditions for revolution are not yet ripe because "the masses" have not yet become convinced of its necessity. The Castroites want a Violent Revolution, sparked by guerrilla warfare in the countryside and a campaign of terrorism, sabotage, and strikes in the cities. They point out that there is no instance of a socialist system having been established without violence, by the Peaceful Road. In some Latin American countries the communists openly say that they prefer the Peaceful Road; in others they quibble by claiming that "the problem of the peaceful or nonpeaceful road primarily depends on the attitude adopted by the ruling classes who are faced with the revolutionary advance of the masses."[7] In any case the communists reject the Cuban thesis that the revolutionaries need not wait until the conditions for revolution are mature but can create these conditions by starting a guerrilla war.[8]

In this debate the Latin American communist parties enjoy the tacit support of the Soviet Union. Even before the Cuban crisis of October 1962, when Soviet policy was still in a highly aggressive phase, the Soviet leaders were reluctant to allow the tempo of their advance into Latin America to be dictated by firebrands like Castro, who often proved unamenable to both reasoning and pressure. The Cuban crisis made the Soviets feel the need for a period of retrenchment and consolidation, that is, Peaceful Coexistence in the sense of a slackening of tension with the United States. Those Latin

[7] *Ibid.*

[8] Thus according to Jorge del Prado in the same article in *Nuestra Epoca:*

> Thus for us, for Peruvian reality, the foreign thesis that in order to light a revolutionary blaze it is sufficient to use the "spark" of a guerrilla nucleus, divorced from the action of the masses and regardless of place and circumstances, is inapplicable. Facing the requirements of the present state of our revolutionary development, and opposed to the adventurous and debilitating policy of those tiny "ultraleftist" groups internationally supported by the Chinese splitters, we advocate an active policy of accumulation of forces.

American communist parties still loyal to Moscow followed suit by moderating their policies, which naturally increased friction with the Castroite extreme nationalists.

The position of the Latin American extreme nationalists thus coincides with that of the Chinese Communists on three vitally important issues: their rejection of the Soviet interpretation of the policy of Peaceful Coexistence as a (possibly only temporary) lessening of tension with the United States, their insistence on an aggressive policy of promoting revolution everywhere, and their rejection of the Soviet thesis of the Peaceful Road to socialism as a mere excuse to avoid revolutionary action.

This triple coincidence does not mean that the Latin American extreme nationalists are Maoists or in any way inspired by Peking. The coincidence arises from a community of political interests: immediate promotion of world revolution regardless of any embarrassment that this action might cause the Soviets, and prevention of any rapprochement between the Soviet Union and the United States. Although it takes place in the general context of the Sino-Soviet dispute, the conflict between the Latin American extreme nationalists and the Latin American communist parties loyal to Moscow was not originated or even sparked by that dispute. The issue at stake is a genuinely Latin American one that would have arisen even if the conflict between Moscow and Peking had not occurred at this precise moment.

Chile is the country in which the debate is being carried on more exhaustively, and can be followed more easily, than anywhere else in Latin America. One reason is that of those Latin American communist parties that have remained in the Soviet fold, the Chilean party is by far the strongest and most influential and frequently acts as spokesman for the rest. Second, the Chilean Communist Party has a worthy debating partner in the almost equally strong and intellectually extremely lively Socialist Party of Chile, which represents the extreme nationalist trend. Third, Chile is a democracy. It has no press or book censorship, and the debate can thus be carried on openly.

Chile is also of especial interest because a third contestant has joined the debate there. An extremely vigorous new mass party, Christian Democracy, is offering peaceful social reform, moderate nationalism, and a "new deal" with the United States as answers to Chile's problems. With this formula it is successfully challenging both the Communists and the Socialists in their strongest bastions.

2

 CHILE—A LATIN AMERICAN
DEMOCRACY[1]

ECONOMIC DIFFICULTIES

Chile is a narrow strip of land 2,800 miles long and
on an average only 110 miles wide along the Pacific
coast of South America. The northernmost thousand
miles are desert and semidesert, the southernmost thousand miles a roadless maze of mountains, glaciers,
fjords, and islands. With the exception of a small minority of Indians, most Chileans are of a fairly uniform
mestizo stock. Ninety per cent of the population
(7,340,000 in 1960) live in the central region, 67 per
cent in the towns and cities, and about 30 per cent in
the capital city of Santiago. Both the birth rate (36 per

[1] The economic and demographic data in this chapter have been
culled from *The South American Handbook, 1962* (38th ed.; London:
Trade and Travel Publications, 1962); Corporación de Fomento de la
Producción, *Geografía económica de Chile*, Vols. III and IV (Santiago
de Chile, 1962); Pedro Cunill's secondary-school *Geografía de Chile*
(Santiago de Chile: Editorial Universitaria, S. A., 1963); and Marvin
J. Sternberg's "Chilean Land Tenure and Land Reform," Ph.D. dis-
sertation, University of California, 1962.

thousand) and the death rate (12.4 per thousand) are extremely high, whereas the illiteracy rate of around 16 per cent of the population over fifteen years of age is one of the lowest in Latin America.

Chile produces about one seventh of the world's copper. Two thirds of her income from exports, which fluctuates between 400 and 550 million dollars per annum, are derived from this metal. According to *The South American Handbook* Chile ranks first among Latin American countries in the production of minerals other than petroleum, in per capita consumption of energy, and in per capita industrial output; second in fisheries; third in literacy; fourth in manufactures, railway mileage, and installed generating capacity; fifth in the number of telephones and radio receivers; sixth in population; seventh in foreign trade; and eighth in size. It is thus one of the most highly developed of these countries. Yet its economy is anything but healthy.

Depreciation of the Chilean currency began as early as 1878; it reached an inflationary rhythm in 1938 and, with brief interruptions, has continued at a frightening pace ever since. There is a great shortage of investment resources; the rate of interest on bank loans is approximately 20 per cent. Industrialization cannot keep pace with the population increase; consequently pressure on the labor market keeps wages down. The distribution of wealth and income is extremely uneven. The big estates of over 2,000 hectares, which are extensively cultivated and render low yields, occupy 60 per cent of the total agricultural area, another 22 per cent of the agricultural area being occupied by holdings of 100–2,000 hectares. On the other end of the scale, 50.1 per cent of all the holdings are of less than 10 hectares, but they occupy only 0.9 per cent of the agricultural area.[2] Distribution of income in the cities and even among wage earners is also most uneven. Wages at the three big American-owned copper mines[3] would be considered reasonable in Europe — averaging around U.S. $180 per month — whereas workers in the small Chilean-owned copper mines make less than one dollar a day. As the agricultural laborers are even worse off than these miners, there is a constant influx into the shantytowns surrounding the cities. Under the circumstances it is not surprising that according to an International Labour Office statistic 50 per cent of all Chileans suffer from malnutrition.[4] Josué de Castro[5] ranks Chile among those Latin American countries that belong to the zone of "extremely defective alimentation, in which quantitative hunger is combined with qualitative insufficiencies of diet."

A RECORD OF POLITICAL STABILITY

Most of these evils are not new; Chile has been suffering from them for several decades. One would expect such a country to have a history of violence and extreme political instability. The opposite is true. Chile's record of political stability is excellent by Latin American and good by even European standards. In the more than one hundred and thirty years that have passed since the consolidation of the Chilean state it has seen less civil

[2] Agricultural census of 1955.

[3] Anaconda's Chuquicamata and El Salvador, and Kennecott's El Teniente.

[4] *The South American Handbook, op. cit.*, p. 357.

[5] See his *Geopolítica del hambre: ensayo sobre los problemas alimentarios y demográficos del mundo* (Buenos Aires: Ediciones Solar and Librería Hachette, S. A., 1962), p. 125.

strife and revolution than France, Germany, or Italy. In Latin America two countries with a considerably higher general living standard, better social conditions, a rather less inequitable distribution of wealth, and an even more numerous and economically more powerful middle class than Chile, namely Argentina and Cuba, have been politically far less stable. This certainly disproves the widely held view that democratic stability is the natural result of general well-being and a strong middle class.

The stability of the democratic regime in Chile is to be attributed not to economic and sociological factors but to something so completely intangible as mere tradition. Democracy was established in nineteenth-century Chile under social conditions very different from those prevailing today. It was an aristocratic democracy with very restricted suffrage and almost complete control of the voting process by the government machine. Yet even in this most imperfect form six decades of uninterrupted democratic — or pseudodemocratic — rule sufficed to establish a firm political tradition.

Most Chilean historians consider the establishment of a stable system of government in nineteenth-century Chile to have been the achievement of one man of genius — the conservative statesman Diego Portales (1793–1837), who conceived the idea of an abstract, impersonal, republican state authority in replacement of the authority of the Spanish crown.[6] Yet they fail to

[6] For Diego Portales, see, among others: Francisco A. Encina and Leopoldo Castedo, *Resumen de la historia de Chile* (4th ed.; Santiago de Chile: Empresa Editora Zig-Zag, S. A., 1961), Vol. II; Alberto Edwards Vives, *La fronda aristocrática* (Santiago de Chile: Editorial Del Pacífico, S. A., 1959); and Hugo Guerra Baeza, *Portales y Rosas: contrapunto de hombres y políticas* (Santiago de Chile: Editorial Del Pacífico, S. A., 1958).

explain how it was possible for this new authority to assert itself and impress itself on the minds of a proud and individualistic people. For once at least the reason is probably to be found in the realm of sheer geography and not in that of political science or ideology.

All along the narrow strip of land that is Chile, and separated from the main centers of population only by a low coastal range, there runs a splendid line of communication — the Pacific Ocean — that enabled the government to maintain constant contact with the outlying provinces. If some provincial caudillo or garrison chief started an insurrection, the Pacific waterway made possible a rapid concentration of troops against him,[7] and if he was defeated in battle, the peculiar configuration of the country prevented him from slipping away to recuperate; there was no remote and inaccessible jungle or mountain fastness to which he could retreat. No other nineteenth-century Latin American country afforded geographical conditions so favorable to the maintenance of a strong centralized system of government. From the middle of the nineteenth century onward the Chilean government strengthened its hold on the country by the construction of a state-owned railroad system, one of the earliest in Latin America; but naval power remained decisive. The only victorious insurrection was the revolution of 1891, when part of the fleet defected, giving the insurgents naval superiority.

But by that time the democratic tradition was already

---

[7] For an eye-witness account of the 1859 Pedro León Gallo rising, which clearly demonstrates the use of naval transportation by the government forces, see the mining prospector Paul Treutler's *Andanzas de un alemán en Chile, 1851–1863* (Santiago de Chile: Editorial Del Pacífico, S. A., 1958).

firmly established; the 1891 revolution was directed against a dictatorial president, Balmaceda, and its object was to restore democratic constitutional government. Balmaceda was a Chilean nationalist who planned to curb the nitrate monopoly set up by the British capitalist J. T. North, to nationalize the nitrate mining companies' private railroads, and to invest in public utilities the annuities that the nitrate companies were obliged to pay to the Chilean state. The insurrection that broke out against him in January 1891 was led by the aristocratic chieftains of the conservative parties and by J. T. North's Chilean lawyer. The government press incessantly harped on this theme, but public opinion remained overwhelmingly in favor of the insurgents and against the president who had dared to violate the constitution.[8]

Left-of-center elements participated in the democratic revolution of 1891, but its ringleaders were the representatives of the aristocratic landowning, mining, and banking interests — in short, the so-called oligarchy. This may seem strange to North Americans and even more to Europeans, who are not accustomed to see the very rich in the role of champions of democracy. But European standards are not valid in Latin America. In such countries as Chile, Argentina, and Brazil the oligarchy has traditionally used democratic institutions as its instruments of rule, not of course without resorting to such procedures as intimidation and the buying of votes. On the other hand, the dictatorial regimes of such authoritarian politicians as Vargas in Brazil, Perón

[8] For the 1891 revolution see Encina and Castedo, *op. cit.*, Vol. III, pp. 1721–1896, and Edwards Vives, *op. cit.*, pp. 151–170.

in Argentina, Ibáñez in Chile — and also of Balmaceda, who in some regards was their precursor — had a definite antioligarchic tendency.

During the three decades of untrammeled parliamentarian rule that followed the revolution of 1891 the oligarchy dominated the scene. Throughout this period governmental and legislative activity was paralyzed by factional strife that led to innumerable cabinet crises. One historian[9] has compared the conditions prevailing in the Chilean parliament of the time with those in the Polish Sejm under the rule of Liberum Veto. But Chile could afford ineffective government. It was not threatened by any external enemy, and the prosperity of the ruling classes and of the state was assured by the revenues paid by the British nitrate monopoly.

The system finally broke down under the double impact of the post-World War I depression and the collapse of the market for natural nitrate, which was brought about by the German invention of synthetic nitrates. In 1920 the popular demagogue Arturo Alessandri was swept to power on a wave of discontent. The traditional parties of the oligarchy were not willing to accept defeat and used their majority position in the parliament to sabotage Alessandri's program of reforms. As a result the president's authority was undermined, and in 1924 he was forced to resign by a military junta. He returned triumphantly the next year to introduce a new constitution establishing presidential supremacy over the parliament, but he was subsequently pushed aside by an ambitious cavalry officer, Colonel Ibáñez, who ruled the country dictatorially until 1931. It is

[9] Edwards Vives, *ibid.*, p. 192.

significant that this period of about six years was by far the longest period of dictatorial government in Chile's entire history as an independent state, and that its end was brought about not by an organized conspiracy but by a mere breakdown of authority that resulted in a series of spontaneous riots.

There followed a year of political anarchy that reached its peak when the commander of the air force, Colonel Marmaduke Grove, staged a military coup in order to proclaim Chile a Socialist Republic. But late in 1932 Alessandri was again elected president, and since then Chile has enjoyed uninterrupted democratic government.

President Arturo Alessandri during his second term of office, which lasted from 1932 to 1938, attempted to rule with the support of a broad coalition of democratic parties ranging from the Conservatives to the middle-class left-of-center Radicals. But the conflict of interests proved too sharp. The two traditional parties of the oligarchy, the Conservatives and Liberals, strove to regain the full control of the state machinery that they had lost through Alessandri's first assumption of the presidency in 1920.[10] The Radicals, seeking to consummate the middle-class revolution of 1920 by winning control of the presidency, left the government coalition and joined forces with the Communists and Socialists in a Popular Front.

The surprise victory of the Radical leader Pedro Aguirre Cerda as Popular Front candidate in the presidential election of 1938 spelled the beginning of a new

[10] In 1920 Alessandri had come to power as the leader of a dissident leftist faction of the Liberals. He became reconciled with the bulk of the Liberal Party in 1931.

era in Chilean politics — that of the undisputed rule of the middle class. Aguirre Cerda's government purged the administrative machinery of representatives of the oligarchy, substituting for them staunch Radicals, and speeded up the industrialization of the country by creating the state-controlled Corporación de Fomento. It is as a result of his improvement and enlargement of the school system that Chile has one of the lowest illiteracy rates in South America. When Aguirre Cerda died in 1942 he was succeeded by another representative of the Radical Party, Juan Antonio Ríos, who came to power with the electoral support of the Socialists and Communists. The third Radical president, Gabriel González Videla, won the election of 1946 with the support of the Radicals and Communists alone. His first cabinet included three Communist ministers, but he broke with the Communists in the following year and after some hesitation banned their party and forced it into clandestinity.

The rapid process of industrialization, which had first been stimulated by the shortages suffered during World War II, continued throughout the 1940's and well into the 1950's. It led to the formation of new urban middle-class and working-class strata, while at the same time the paternalistic relations between the landowners and their agricultural laborers began to disintegrate. In the political life of the country these social changes were reflected by the emergence of a large body of voters not linked with and not attracted by the traditional parties of the Right, Center, and Left.

In the presidential election of 1952 the support of such floating voters, increased by sizable defections from the traditional parties, gave victory to the former dictator Carlos Ibáñez, who had spent the last two decades in a relentless struggle to stage a comeback. Ibáñez had inspired several military conspiracies, had allied himself with the fascists and at the same time negotiated with the Popular Front in the 1930's, and in 1942 had unsuccessfully run for president as the candidate of the oligarchic parties. In 1952 he presented himself as the enemy of the oligarchy and of a corrupt parliamentary regime; his propaganda took its cues from the Argentinian dictator Juan Perón, then at the height of his prestige throughout Latin America. But once in power, Ibáñez, grown prudent with age, disappointed those of his followers who had expected him to install a Justicialist regime on the Argentinian pattern. Political conditions were very different from those that had enabled him to establish his dictatorship in 1925. In 1952 the country was not in an institutional crisis, democracy was firmly entrenched, and the army chieftains were determined to respect the constitutional order. Since Ibáñez did not feel strong enough to force a showdown with the parliament, in which he did not control a majority, he was obliged to temporize. His period of administration was thus characterized by improvisation and incessant changes in the personnel of his cabinet. By the end of his presidential period in 1958, his prestige and influence were no longer sufficient to ensure the victory of the candidate whom he favored in that year's presidential election, Salvador Allende of the FRAP (Frente de Acción Popular) coalition of Socialists and Communists. The candidate of the Liberals and Conservatives, Arturo Alessandri's son Jorge, won the election by a narrow margin.

President Jorge Alessandri gave the country a six-year period of political stability and efficient administration. Vast housing and road-building programs were implemented, and the damage caused by the earthquake that devastated large areas of southern Chile in 1960 was quickly repaired. His rectitude and austerity appealed to the people; his popularity increased throughout his term of office. Yet Chile's basic problems remained unsolved. In spite of determined efforts, Alessandri could not halt inflation. Under his administration Chile's foreign debt reached unprecedented heights, but the investment programs financed with foreign loans failed to revive the rate of growth, which had declined to less than 3 per cent per annum in the last years of the previous administration.

The stagnation of economic development was not due simply to errors in government policy. Its root cause lay deeper: It was that the internal market was too small to encourage or absorb a further expansion of industrial production; and this fundamental weakness in the economy was due to the existence of a vast rural and urban subproletariat living at a mere subsistence level. With the increasing awareness of this situation, and in spite of Alessandri's personal popularity, those groups that condemned his conservative policies and advocated changes in the country's social and economic structure as the only solution to Chile's plight grew ever stronger as his term of office drew to its close.

THE CHILEAN POLITICAL SYSTEM

The Chilean constitution provides for the separation of powers. Executive power is vested in a president, who is elected by popular vote. The president is not dependent on a parliamentary majority, and the only constitutional possibility of removing him from office before the expiration of his term is by a difficult process of impeachment. Members of parliament cannot join his cabinet without waiving their mandate; technically, cabinet members are presidential aides, though in fact they may function as the representatives of a political party.

The legislative power, or parliament, is composed of two chambers, the Senate, whose members are elected for a term of eight years, and a Chamber of Deputies, which has a four-year term. The president is elected for a six-year term and cannot succeed himself in office. Presidential elections are traditionally held in even years, for instance, 1946, 1952, 1958, 1964, whereas parliamentary elections (for the Chamber of Deputies and one half of the Senate) are held in uneven years, 1953, 1957, 1961, 1965. The presidential and parliamentary elections are thus never scheduled for the same year.

Illiterates are not entitled to the vote, the test of literacy being the ability to write one's own name. Male and female voters use separate polling booths, and their votes are counted separately, thus providing a unique opportunity to ascertain differences of political opinion between the sexes. Thus it was established that President Alessandri owed his victory in the 1958 election to the female vote, a majority of the male voters having preferred the leftist candidate Allende.

The presidential candidates are usually nominated by political parties; no independent candidate has ever been elected president without the backing of at least one political community of some standing and numerical strength.

The seven major political parties in Chile today, moving from right to left in the political spectrum, are

1. The Conservative Party is one of the two parties of the aristocratic oligarchy that ruled Chile throughout the nineteenth and well into the twentieth century. It was formerly officially recognized as the party of the Catholic Church and as such could count on substantial popular support. As late as 1949 it polled 22 per cent of the total vote.[11] Since then it has lost heavily, first to the ephemeral nationalist parties supporting the caudillo Ibáñez, then to the Christian Democrats and the Liberals. In the municipal elections of 1963 the Conservatives polled 11.35 per cent of the valid votes.

2. The Liberals are the second traditional party of the aristocratic oligarchy. Although their basic doctrines are diametrically opposed, the practical policies of the Liberals and the Conservatives coincide. Both stand for the defense of property and private enterprise and for close alliance with the United States. Both are opposed to state intervention and are violently anti-communist.[12] In the 1963 municipal elections the Liberals polled 13.02 per cent of the valid votes.

3. The Radical Party was founded in 1863 by a group of militantly anticlerical Santiago intellectuals and provincial oligarchs. It later became the party of the nascent Chilean middle class, even though to this day it has a conservative wing of big landowners. In

[11] The data on the relative strength of the Chilean political parties are taken from Sergio Guilisasti Tagle's book, *Partidos políticos chilenos* (2nd ed., enlarged; Santiago de Chile: Editorial Nascimento, 1964).

[12] This did not prevent the Liberals from participating in President Gabriel González Videla's first government (1946–1947), which included three Communist members.

Chile as in other Latin American countries middle-class opinion is predominantly nationalist, interventionist, and protectionist; it is in favor of strong social legislation and of state measures to promote new industries in order to cut down unemployment, increase the buying power of the masses, and create new opportunities for the administrative and technical intelligentsia. These middle-class postulates are reflected in the program and policies of the Radical Party. Another important feature of Chilean Radicalism is its militant anticlericalism. The spirit of Voltaire is still very strong in this party, as evinced by the welcoming words of the Radical Julio Durán, then Speaker of the Chamber of Deputies, to the International Congress of Christian Democrats held in Santiago in 1955:

We are not Christians but are prepared to give up our lives in order that Christianity, as all other religious and political creeds, shall be accorded free and sovereign expression in the Americas and in the entire world.[13]

[13] Quoted from *Congresos Internacionales Demócrata-Cristianos* (Santiago de Chile: Editorial Del Pacífico, S. A., 1957), p. 112. The apparent anachronism of a political party still swayed by the spirit of eighteenth-century rationalism in the middle of the twentieth century is a product of Chile's specific historical development. Up to the year 1810 Chile had been one of the most remote colonies of a country that had experienced only feeble reflections of the Renaissance and the Enlightenment. In the early years of the republic the teachings of European rationalism were known to only a handful of individuals who soon lost all influence and were pushed into impotent opposition by the conservative regime. But by the second half of the nineteenth century, Chile, as the world's largest copper producer, was closely linked with Europe — far more closely than it is today. It was only then, some fifty years after her political liberation, that Chile's cultural emancipation from Spain took place. It took the form of a belated discovery of French eighteenth-century rationalism: The educated public now took cognizance of the writings of Voltaire, Rousseau, and the Encyclopedists. By that time the country was in the throes of a conflict between Church and state that was not settled

For the last half century the Radical Party has steadily polled around 20 per cent of the total vote and occupied a key position in the Chilean parliament, thus making it difficult to form a government without its assistance. From 1938 to 1952 three Radicals in succession occupied the presidency,[14] which commands the levers of patronage. In consequence the Radicals are firmly entrenched in the administrative machinery and the big state-owned enterprises. In addition to the old conservative group of big landowners the party has thus acquired a powerful new right wing of financiers, contractors, managers, and senior civil servants all interested in the maintenance of the status quo. There is great tension between these elements and the doctrinaire left wing, and the party is held together only by the discipline imposed by a highly centralized machine. In the municipal elections of 1963 the Radical Party polled 21.59 per cent of the valid votes.

4. The Chilean Christian Democrats are a leftist party. Their program of drastic social reform and "assertive nationalism" has broad popular appeal. Their supporters include middle-class elements who, being Catholics, have been excluded from the patronage dispensed by the anticlerical Radical Party, technicians, office workers, a minority of organized labor, and a large and devoted following among the urban subproletariat of the *callampas* (shantytowns).[15] The Christian Demo-

until 1925. The nascent Chilean middle class and its political cadres were thus formed in a climate of rationalism and anticlericalism — a heritage that is still potent today.

[14] These were Presidents Pedro Aguirre Cerda (1938–1942) and Juan Antonio Ríos (1942–1946), each of whom died in the fourth year of his six-year term, and Gabriel González Videla (1946–1952).

[15] The cities and larger towns of Chile are surrounded by shantytown districts called *callampas* (that is, mushrooms), which are in-

crats have also gradually acquired a fringe of financiers and industrialists, but these are self-made men and not members of the established oligarchy. The party is led by a group of Catholic intellectuals inspired by the Christian social political philosophy of Jacques Maritain. In the municipal elections of 1963 the Christian Democrats polled 22.8 per cent of the valid votes, thus overtaking the Radicals to become Chile's strongest political party.

5. The backbone of the Socialist Party is formed by the better-paid categories of organized labor such as the workers in the big American-owned copper mines, the marine workers, and railroad workers. But the party also has a following among other sectors of the working class, including the urban subproletariat of the *callampas* and the desperately poor agricultural laborers, as well as among technicians, school teachers, and professionals. The Socialists are the party of those who are attracted by the doctrine of proletarian revolution but reject Communist leadership and mental discipline. They are not a social democratic party. Their leaders point with pride to the fact that they are not a member party of the Socialist International. They have a record of participation in military conspiracies and coups. Although they are not so sectarian as to reject its practical benefits, their attitude toward parliamentary democracy is negative in principle. It is well characterized by the following editorial statement of their theoretical review *Arauco:*

The defense of democracy is only this cynical game: to impel the acceptance of the existing social and economic

---

habited by a subproletariat of unskilled workers who have drifted in from the rural areas.

order, with all its misery, frustrations, and contrasts, through the respect for symbols that are declared to be eternal and are then identified with anachronistic social and economic structures.[16]

The Chilean Socialists are also remarkable for their ideological instability. In the brief space of thirty years they have been militant anticommunists, members of a Communist-sponsored Popular Front, admirers of the Argentinian fascist regime of Juan Perón, Titoists, and enthusiastic Castroites. Of late their left wing has developed pro-Chinese tendencies. The one factor that has remained constant throughout these changes is their fervent Latin-American nationalism, which is of the extreme, highly anti-American brand. Their attitude toward the Communists, with whom they are linked in an uneasy alliance, is one of dislike and distrust. In the municipal elections of 1963 the Socialists polled 11.48 per cent of the valid votes.

6. The Chilean Communist Party is the strongest and best-organized communist party in South America. It is far more firmly rooted in the working class than most of its Latin American fellow parties, its main base being the workers of Chile's largest industry, mining.[17] The Communists also have a following among writers and artists,[18] but in general Chilean leftist intellectuals appear to much prefer the Socialists. In the municipal elections of 1963 the Communists polled 12.8 per cent of the valid votes.

[16] *Arauco*, No. 49, February 1964.
[17] With the exception of the workers of the "Gran Minería," the large American-owned copper mines, who are predominantly Socialist.
[18] Pablo Neruda, who is Latin America's greatest literary figure, and may well be the world's greatest living poet, is a member of the Chilean Communist Party's Politburo.

7. The Chilean political scene includes smaller parties without any effective organization that rarely survive for more than one election. At present the most important of these is the Partido Democrático Nacional (PADENA), composed of followers of that typical Latin American caudillo, the late President Ibáñez. The PADENA polled 5.3 per cent of the valid votes in the 1963 municipal elections.

Both the Right and the Left have a lunatic fringe of tiny extremist groups, National Socialists and Fascists on the Right, various brands of Trotskyites, Pekingites, and Castroites on the Left.[19] None of these sects has numerous followers or is organizationally strong enough to carry any weight in an electoral contest.

[19] The ultraleftist parties are briefly described in the Appendix.

3

THE COMMUNIST PARTY OF CHILE
AND THE POLICY OF THE
PEACEFUL ROAD

THE POPULAR FRONT POLICY OF
BROAD ALLIANCES WITH LIMITED AIMS

The lack of revolutionary dynamism characteristic of Latin American communist parties in general is very evident in the history of the Communist Party of Chile, although it is the strongest and best organized of them all. Even in the wild days of its youth, when it was in the grip of third period ultraradicalism,[1] the Chilean party's revolutionary record was undistinguished. Its highlights were an attack on a provincial army barracks by a band of party members, and a Central Committee decision to support a naval mutiny that had been started without the party's knowledge.[2]

Both events occurred after the downfall of President Ibáñez in 1931, in a period of confusion of which the

[1] This period lasted roughly from 1929 to 1935.
[2] See Robert J. Alexander, *Communism in Latin America* (New Brunswick, N.J.: Rutgers University Press, 1957), pp. 185 f.

Communists did not otherwise take advantage. In 1932, when asked by Marmaduke Grove and his Socialist friends to join in the preparations for the June 4 military rising that was to install a Socialist Republic, they refused to participate. During the June revolution itself they denounced the revolutionaries as "a sector of the bourgeoisie allied to imperialism."[3]

The ultraleftist third period strategy of which this was an example aimed at the destruction of the social democratic parties, which were declared to be the main obstacles on the road to Violent Revolution and to the formation of Russian-type workers', peasants', and soldiers' soviets.[4] The strategy had no relation whatsoever to Chilean reality. It was thus rejected by the Chilean workers, and the Communist Party was reduced to the status of a small sect.

Communist fortunes were restored through the efforts of Eudocio Ravines, a brilliant Peruvian communist party organizer who was sent to Chile in 1935 by the Comintern headquarters in Moscow.[5] Ravines' Chilean assignment was to implement the new United Front and antifascist Popular Front strategy that had replaced the ultraleftist third period strategy as the official line of the Comintern.[6]

---

[3] *Ibid.*, pp. 186 f.

[4] Thus the French Communists' slogan throughout the period was *"Les soviets partout!"*

[5] See Eudocio Ravines' autobiographical book, *La gran estafa* (4th ed.; Santiago de Chile: Editorial Del Pacífico, S. A., 1957). An early study of the Popular Front era in Chile, written when it was not yet possible to foresee the experiment's inglorious end, is John Reese Stevenson's *The Chilean Popular Front* (Philadelphia: University of Pennsylvania Press, 1942).

[6] In some communist parties, the swing away from third period ultraleftism had started as early as 1934, but the United Front and Popular Front policies became official and obligatory Comintern strategy only after the Seventh World Congress in 1935.

The new Popular Front policy, which aimed at a broad alliance of Marxist and non-Marxist parties in order to "stop fascism," at first glance appeared to have as little rapport with Chilean reality as the ultraleftism of the previous period. Only a few years before, the Ibáñez dictatorship had ignominiously collapsed. After a year of troubles, democracy had triumphantly returned to Chile and was then firmly established under the constitutional rule of President Alessandri. This democratic president and the right-of-center coalition of Liberals and Conservatives that supported him were the real opponents of the Chilean Left. The small, albeit vociferous Chilean Nazi Party led by González von Marées was only a minor threat. It is true that the Chilean Nazis enjoyed the backing of ex-dictator Ibáñez, who was utterly unscrupulous and indiscriminate in his choice of the instruments through which he hoped to come back to power. Yet Ibáñez was not regarded as a "fascist danger" by the Left. He had many sympathizers in the Radical and Socialist parties, and at one stage even the Communists considered him for the Popular Front's presidential candidate in 1938.

As has already been pointed out, European political terminology is applied in Chile to conditions differing greatly from those encountered in Europe. This is a source of confusion not only to foreign observers but frequently also to the Chileans themselves. Many supporters of the Chilean Popular Front certainly pictured themselves as fighting a heroic battle to save their country from fascism.[7] Yet fascism or antifascism was

[7] See, for instance, the passionate antifascism of Marta Vergara in her book, *Memorias de una mujer irreverente* (Santiago de Chile: Empresa Editora Zig-Zag, S. A., 1962).

not the real issue in the Chilean Popular Front campaign of the late 1930's. This is dramatically illustrated by the events that led to the victory of the Popular Front presidential candidate Pedro Aguirre Cerda in 1938.

On the morning of September 5, 1938 a band of young Chilean Nazis of González von Marées' party seized the University of Chile building and the building of the Labor Insurance office (Caja de Seguro Obrero) in the immediate vicinity of the presidential palace after cold-bloodedly killing a policeman on guard. The support that they had expected from the Santiago garrison did not materialize, and the sixty-two Nazi insurgents were soon forced to surrender to police reinforcements. Later their battered corpses were found in the Seguro Obrero building. The police, enraged by the murder of their comrade, had slaughtered all but one.

Strangely enough, Chilean public opinion at the time regarded — and to this day regards — this typical Nazi coup on the model of the Vienna Ballhausplatz coup in 1934 as a pardonable expression of youthful high spirits, whereas the killing of the perpetrators caused a wave of indignation to sweep the country. A plaque commemorating the sixty-two young martyrs now decorates the front of the Seguro Obrero building facing the presidential palace, and Chileans of all political denominations still regard the "massacre of the Caja del Seguro," as it is called, as a stain on the record of President Alessandri. This does not mean that the Chileans are profascist but simply that, not having gone through the horrors of World War II, they do not have the same strong emotional reaction to fascism as Europeans and North Americans.

In protest against the massacre, González von Marées and his ally, ex-dictator Ibáñez, appealed to their supporters to vote for the Popular Front in the coming presidential election, and there is no doubt that this support was decisive in the election, by a very narrow margin, of the Popular Front candidate, the Radical leader Pedro Aguirre Cerda. In his autobiography the veteran Communist Elías Lafertte claims that Aguirre Cerda himself visited Ibáñez in jail[8] in order to close the deal by which he obtained the fascist vote in return for the promise of an amnesty.

The 1938 election victory of the allegedly antifascist Popular Front was thus obtained with fascist support. Nor did the Popular Front display any great antifascist ardor after it had safely installed itself in power. Thus Chile never declared war on Germany in spite of the fact that throughout World War II it was governed by Popular Front presidents supported by the Communists. Pro-German sentiment was strong in the ruling Radical Party and was shared by both wartime presidents, Pedro Aguirre Cerda (1938–1942) and Juan Antonio Ríos (1942–1946).[9] Both presidents were staunch democrats, and their German sympathies stemmed from admiration for the country, not for its regime. But some government circles were not immune to Nazi ideological influence. Thus Aguirre Cerda's Minister of the Interior in 1941, Arturo Olavarría Bravo, first obliged the Jewish community of Santiago to pay

[8] See Elías Lafertte, *Vida de un comunista (páginas autobiográficas)* (Santiago de Chile: Talleres Gráficos Horizonte, 1961), p. 313.

[9] President Ríos, much to his regret, did see himself obliged to break off diplomatic relations with Germany and to declare war on Germany's ally Japan.

for the installation of the city's traffic-light system and then worked out a project to have all Jewish immigrants who were engaged in commerce deported to the remote southern province of Chiloé. In his autobiography[10] Olavarría quite proudly relates all this, claiming that his deportation project was approved by the two parliamentary representatives of Chiloé province, Exequiel González Madariaga and Héctor Correa Letelier, and that he was prevented from implementing it only by having to resign for other reasons.[11]

Since Chileans invariably employ European political terminology, their Popular Front alliance of left-of-center parties paraded as an alliance to defend democracy against fascism. But as we have seen, this was only a façade. In reality antifascist sentiment was certainly not strong enough, and the threat of German domination far too remote, to provide the basis of a political alliance. That the Popular Front formula proved successful in Chile in spite of this is to be attributed to a purely Chilean cause that had little

[10] Arturo Olavarría Bravo, *Chile entre dos Alessandri: memorias políticas*, 2 vols. (Santiago de Chile: Editorial Nascimento, 1962).

[11] *Ibid.*, Vol. I, pp. 486 ff. On the other hand the same Olavarría effectively disposed of the Chilean Nazi Party by having the Nazi leader Gonzáles von Marées taken to a mental hospital for examination. The Nazi leader soon obtained his release, but, according to Olavarría (*ibid.*, Vol. I, p. 527), he could never rid himself of the stigma of having been considered "loco," and his movement soon withered away. Olavarría had been the Popular Front campaign manager in 1938. After the war he organized an anticommunist militia armed with rifles and machine guns. In 1952 he served as campaign manager for Carlos Ibáñez, who won the presidential election of that year. In 1958 he served Jorge Alessandri in a similar capacity, and in 1964 he was the campaign manager for Salvador Allende, candidate of the Socialist-Communist FRAP coalition. European political concepts and terminology evidently do not suffice to explain the intricacies of Chilean politics.

to do with ideology and nothing whatsoever to do with the international situation. The real basis for the construction of the Popular Front in Chile was merely the slightly left-of-center Radical Party's desperate urge to obtain control of government patronage and the Communists' willingness to help them do so.

Founded in 1863 by a group of militantly anticlerical oligarchs, the Chilean Radicals had gradually evolved into a party of white-collar workers, schoolteachers, small industrialists, and farmers. By the 1930's they were the strongest and best-organized political group in Chile, but they had never occupied the presidency. The power to dispense government patronage on a large scale had remained with the two traditional parties, the Liberals and the Conservatives, that is, with the aristocratic clans. The position occupied by the Radical Party during the second administration of President Arturo Alessandri (1932–1938) is vividly described by Eudocio Ravines:

> While the party collaborated with the Alessandri government, the Conservatives and Liberals disposed of all the government posts, of the best positions in the state institutions, of the so-called "Grand Duke" salaries in the civil service. The Radicals wasted their prestige, wore themselves out politically, and wiped their mouths while their Liberal and Conservative colleagues ate and drank. And there was a sullen murmur of discontent in vast sectors of Radicalism.[12]

The Communists therefore did not find it too difficult to woo the Radical Party into the Popular Front with the slogan: "The next President of Chile shall be a Radical!"

[12] Ravines, *op. cit.*, pp. 103 f.

This slogan summarized the real purpose of the Chilean Popular Front: It was nothing more than an alliance formed in order to enable the Radicals to seize the presidency and thus obtain control of government patronage. Of course similar considerations also played their part in European Popular Front movements, but besides this, in countries such as France and Spain, the Popular Front parties, including the Communists, shared a real sense of the need to defend republican and democratic institutions against the imminent threat of rightist dictatorship. As far as the Communists were concerned, this was not due to a genuine conversion to the principle of parliamentary democracy but to the fact that Moscow, after the fall of the Weimar Republic, had belatedly come to realize that it was in its interests at least temporarily to back democratic governments in other European countries in order to prevent the spread of fascism in Western Europe.

There was none of this in the Chilean Popular Front. In Chile President Alessandri and the right-of-center parties defended the democratic institutions, while even before the Seguro Obrero massacre the Popular Front parties had conducted an outrageous flirtation with ex-dictator Ibáñez, who constituted the only real threat to Chilean democracy.

The Chilean Radicals had every reason to be satisfied with the result of their alliance with the Marxist parties. Thanks to the Popular Front, a Radical was elected president for the first time in the history of Chile. Pedro Aguirre Cerda's victory in the 1938 election enabled the Radicals to obtain all those important positions and "Grand Duke" salaries that had hitherto been monopolized by the Liberals and Conservatives.

In accordance with the general principles of Popular Front strategy as laid down by the Seventh World Congress of the Comintern in 1935, the Communists did not participate in President Pedro Aguirre Cerda's government, although they did lend it their parliamentary support.[13] Nor did they benefit from government patronage. President Aguirre Cerda's way of dealing with them is amusingly described in the veteran Communist Elías Lafertte's autobiography:

On assuming office, Aguirre Cerda asked the Communist Party to nominate ministers, but the party declined to participate in the cabinet. It would give the government total support, but from without. The president then asked us for a list with the names of comrades who could occupy posts in the public administration. The list was handed in, the candidates were enthusiastically approved by Don Pedro, but none of them was nominated.[14]

The Communists thus obtained only limited indirect benefits from their participation in the Popular Front. The most important of these was that their association with the powerful non-Marxist Radical Party gave them respectability and status in Chilean politics. To some degree they had already enjoyed this position in the early 1920's, the first years of their existence, but it had been completely gambled away through the irresponsibility of their third period extremism. By their apparently disinterested contribution to the victory of Pedro Aguirre Cerda, who was a millionaire wine grower and the leader of the right wing of the Radical Party, they showed the ambitious professionals of

[13] The rule of nonparticipation in Popular Front governments was broken only in Spain, under the pressure of the Civil War.

[14] *Op. cit.*, p. 316.

Chilean politics that they could be useful and that it was worth while to cultivate their acquaintance. They became a force to be reckoned with, a regular participant in the intricate game of Chilean politics, and have remained so ever since.

Such was the result of the Communists' participation in the Popular Front, but it hardly explains why they initiated it. In 1936, the year in which they began their Popular Front drive, they could scarcely have foreseen how enormously this policy would improve their status. Furthermore the desire for respectability has never been a prime motive in the policies of any communist party. Their real reason for launching the Popular Front had nothing to do with Chile; it was simply that they had been ordered to do so by Moscow. In 1935 the Popular Front had become the general line of the international communist movement, to which all communist parties had to adhere. Every single one of them followed that line, but most failed in their efforts because the socialist and left-of-center non-Marxist parties refused to cooperate. The Chilean Communists were exceptionally lucky in encountering conditions that actually permitted the formation of a durable Popular Front alliance. By their success they greatly improved their standing within the Comintern, and to their leaders this probably seemed far more important than the attainment of respectability in Chile itself.

That the Chilean Popular Front was not really anti-fascist and that it had won the 1938 election with the help of the fascist vote did not matter very much since Chile was so remote that Moscow would probably not notice this insignificant detail. In 1938 the Soviets had far more important things to worry about than the political situation in a faraway Latin American country. They were weak and completely on the defensive and could not even dream about establishing a base many thousands of miles away on the American continent. The importance of the Chilean Popular Front to them was purely propagandistic; its success offered additional proof of the efficacy of the Popular Front policy and encouraged communist parties in more important parts of the world to increase their efforts.

THE PERIOD OF CLANDESTINITY

The Chilean Communists' refusal to participate in the Popular Front government of 1938 is usually attributed to a desire to take credit for the government's successes while remaining free to criticize its failures. But taking into account the peculiar atmosphere prevailing in the international communist movement in the 1930's, one arrives at a simpler and less Machiavellian explanation. At that time Stalin's authority was not yet quite so great and the communist world movement not quite so malleable in his hands as in the postwar period. A whole generation of the leading cadres of the communist parties had been trained in the spirit of third period ultraleftism at the Lenin International Party School in Moscow. For them the Popular Front program of alliance with the detested social democrats and even with bourgeois parties, the cultivation of a patriotic phraseology, and the defense of formal democracy and parliamentary institutions was sheer heresy. To actually postulate or condone communist participation in bourgeois governments — an act that Lenin had regarded as the main crime of the social democrats — would have been more than they could stand.[15]

But the Second World War brought about a measure of collaboration between communist and noncommunist resistance movements in a number of countries. The communist parties became accustomed to Popular Fronts and even wider alliances, and in Italy and France and some other liberated countries they even joined the government. In 1946 the Chilean Communists followed their example.

The government the Communists now joined was that of the Radical Party leader Gabriel González Videla, who had won that year's presidential election with the support of the Communists but not of the Socialists. The Communists were given three ministries — Communications and Public Works, Lands and Colonization, and Agriculture. In order to obtain a parliamentary majority, Gabriel González Videla also had to call in the right-of-center Liberals, whereas the Socialists remained in opposition.

After only five months the three Communist ministers were dismissed from the cabinet. Purely domestic reasons, the arrogant comportment of the Communists and their inroads on the voting strength of their democratic allies in the municipal elections of April 1947, are usually given for their dismissal. But it must be remembered that the Communists' short-lived participation in the government — from December 1946 through April 1947 — coincided with a period of stead-

15 In reading the main speeches of the 1935 Seventh World Congress of the Comintern one will find that they were all designed to placate leftist opposition to the new line by insisting that it did not mean betrayal or even postponement of the revolution.

ily increasing tension between the Soviet Union and the United States and with an about-face of the international communist movement to a militantly anti-American line. Since President González Videla and the two democratic parties of the government coalition, the Radicals and the Liberals, did not intend to strain Chile's relations with the United States, their collaboration with the Communists could not have lasted much longer in any event. It is also significant that at the very moment of joining the government the Communists replaced their Secretary-General Carlos Contreras Labarca, who had been accused of softness toward the United States, with his main critic, Ricardo Fonseca, the advocate of a tough policy.[16]

Having expelled the Communists from his government, President González Videla apparently at first wanted to avoid a complete break with the party, which would have made him dependent on the votes of the right-of-center parties. A Communist source, the memorial volume dedicated to Ricardo Fonseca, states that in August 1947 the President told a delegation of Communist leaders that he hoped to reincorporate them in the cabinet after some time, and that he even asked them "to name some Communists not known as such, whose party affiliation was to be kept strictly secret, so that he could nominate them to the cabinet as his personal friends."[17]

[16] See the memorial volume, *Ricardo Fonseca: combatiente ejemplar,* prepared under the direction of the Secretariat of the Communist Party by the Commission of Historical Studies annexed to its Central Committee (Santiago de Chile: Talleres Gráficos Lautaro [1952]), pp. 130 ff., on Fonseca's struggle against Carlos Contreras Labarca's "Browderism."
[17] *Ibid.,* p. 157.

The offer was rejected, but the Communists still took their exclusion from the government quietly. It was only after several months of hesitation that they opened hostilities against González Videla by launching a series of political strikes. Their decision to do so coincided with the swing of the entire international communist movement to a policy of out-and-out class warfare after the Soviet Union's refusal to participate in the Marshall Plan, and it may thus be doubted that the Chilean party leadership took this step entirely of its own accord.

President González Videla now moved against the Communists. Thousands of party cadres were arrested and many deported to an internment camp, the derelict port of Pisagua on the edge of Chile's bleak northern desert. The next year the parliament passed the Law for the Defense of Democracy, by which the Communist Party was banned and its members were struck from the voters' register.

In the face of this government offensive the Communists adopted a policy of what their historians[18] call "organized, battling retreat" into clandestinity in order to "save the organization and the cadres." But this policy was opposed by a strong sector of the party leadership, headed by organizational secretary Luis Reinoso and the Secretary-General of the Communist Youth, Daniel Palma. The Reinoso-Palma group advocated a policy of terrorism and armed rising. In the words of Luis Corvalán:

Reinoso transformed the National Organizational Commission into a second party leadership. Then he organized a complete semimilitary apparatus for provocations, based

18 *Ibid.*, pp. 166 f.

on the false perspective that the dictatorship of González Videla could be overthrown by an armed rising, and, what is worse, by the action of groups isolated from the masses, composed of party activists, many of whom he persuaded to provocative terrorist actions and useless sacrifices. In this manner Reinoso substituted for the essential communist tactic of always acting in unison with the masses the fruitless struggle of isolated groups of activists who were easy prey for the police. . . .[19]

Late in 1948 the Secretary-General of the party, Ricardo Fonseca, fell seriously ill, and this apparently gave Reinoso the chance to forge ahead with the preparations for an armed rising. Through his henchman Benjamín Cares, who went to Moscow with a party delegation, he even appears temporarily to have obtained Soviet support for his militant policy. In his autobiography the Communist veteran Elías Lafertte states that Cares in the Soviet Union "painted a picture of the Chilean political scene that had nothing to do with reality."[20] Lafertte fails to indicate whether the Soviets rejected this picture; and, since he is always extremely careful not to reveal anything damaging to either side in the relations between Moscow and the Chilean party, one may infer that the Soviets were impressed enough to endorse Reinoso's policy. But in the end those Chilean Communist leaders who advocated less hazardous methods of resistance won out.

According to the party historians a clash between Reinoso and Secretary-General Ricardo Fonseca occurred on the occasion of the March 1948 parliamentary

[19] *El Partido Comunista de Chile y el movimiento comunista internacional: documentos e informes emanados de plenos y congresos del Partido Comunista de Chile* (Santiago de Chile: Empresa Horizonte, [1964]), p. 39.
[20] Lafertte, *op. cit.*, p. 347.

elections, with Reinoso advocating a boycott whereas the party line was to vote for non-Communist candidates opposed to González Videla's policies.[21] But it was only after Fonseca's death in July 1949 that matters came to a head. The new Secretary-General, Galo González, finally had Reinoso, Cares, Palma, and several of their henchmen expelled in a major party purge in 1950. It is indicative of the mood of the Chilean party leadership that Galo González was by no means a member of the right wing of the party but a typical representative of the "obreristas," the tough, anti-intellectual, working-class component of the party.[22]

Meanwhile the government's attitude toward the Communist Party had become somewhat milder. Late in 1949 most of the prisoners and internees were released, and the party, although still banned, was again permitted to function as a political body. The Communists were thus able to participate in the multiple interparty negotiations preceding the 1952 presidential election.

One of the candidates in this election was the former dictator Carlos Ibáñez, who campaigned on a demagogic, antiparliamentarian, and antioligarchic platform. Ibáñez was supported by a motley collection of rightist, semifascist, and left-of-center groups. These included the main body of the Socialist Party, the Partido Socialista Popular, which at this time was under the spell of Peronism and hence greatly attracted by Ibáñez, a personal and political friend of Juan Perón.

For some time the Communists contemplated joining the crowd of Ibáñez supporters. One of their leaders,

[21] See memorial volume, *Ricardo Fonseca, op. cit.*, p. 175.
[22] See Vergara, *op. cit.*, p. 129.

the poet Pablo Neruda, in a press statement even announced the party's support of the ex-dictator,[23] and the party's grand old man, Elías Lafertte, appeared on the platform side by side with Ibáñez at an election meeting.[24] But the party leadership finally decided otherwise and joined with a Socialist splinter group, the Partido Socialista de Chile, in promoting the candidature of that group's representative, Salvador Allende.[25]

This decision was highly significant. The Communists' new ally, the Partido Socialista de Chile, was the most moderate, democratic sector of the socialist movement. It had a record of militant anticommunism, had voted for the Law for the Defense of Democracy, and had supported the González Videla government in its anticommunist phase. In aligning themselves with this group instead of with Ibáñez, who had promised to repeal the Law for the Defense of Democracy, the Communists demonstrated that they preferred the relative safety of parliamentary democracy to the hazards of an antioligarchic, socially progressive experiment in authoritarianism. This choice was all the more remarkable because the Communist leaders were certainly aware that Salvador Allende's candidacy had no chance of success and that its only possible effect would be to draw leftist votes away from Ibáñez. But since the Communists could not possibly vote for either the candidate of the right-of-center Liberals and Conserva-

[23] See Ernesto Würth Rojas, *Ibáñez, caudillo enigmático* (Santiago de Chile: Editorial Del Pacífico, S. A., 1958), p. 226.

[24] See Lafertte, *op. cit.*, p. 347.

[25] Originally Salvador Allende had been with the Partido Socialista Popular, but he had seceded and joined the splinter group when his party had decided to support Ibáñez.

tives or the Radical candidate, who was a personal friend of González Videla, Allende was the only democratic candidate whom they could support. In choosing Allende over Ibáñez the Communists were evidently trying to work their way back into the democratic establishment from which they had been cast out five years before.

In the event, Ibáñez won the election by an overwhelming margin. During the six years of his term of office the Communists consistently opposed him. In the later years of this period the majority group of the Socialists, whose expectations had been disappointed by Ibáñez, joined them. The two Socialist groups, the Partido Socialista Popular and the Partido Socialista de Chile, then reunited and together with the Communists formed the FRAP alliance. The Communists at first hoped to expand FRAP into a Popular Front by including the Radicals or Christian Democrats, but their Socialist allies blocked this move. Even so, the FRAP candidate in the 1958 presidential election, again Salvador Allende, came in second, a mere 40,000 votes behind the victorious candidate of the right-of-center parties, and left the candidates of the Christian Democrats and the Radicals far behind. Before turning over the office to his successor, President Ibáñez repealed the Law for the Defense of Democracy, thus restoring the Communist Party to full legality.

THE POLICY OF THE PEACEFUL ROAD TO SOCIALISM

Meanwhile the international communist movement had been shaken by a momentous event. In 1956 the Twentieth Congress of the Soviet Communists had revealed a number of Stalin's crimes, and it had also repealed two fundamental doctrines of Leninism. In view of the increased strength of the "socialist camp" and other "forces of peace," Lenin's doctrine of the inevitability of war was declared no longer valid. And the doctrine of the inevitability of Violent Revolution was replaced by the statement that socialism, in view of the growing strength of the "popular forces," could in some countries come to power by the Peaceful Road.

As we have seen, the Chilean Communists had already practiced the policy of the Peaceful Road for over twenty years. Even in the time of their persecution by González Videla they had expelled the advocates of armed insurrection from their ranks. Ideologically they had justified this policy with the argument that the masses were not yet ready for revolution and that Lenin had declared it to be a stupidity and a crime to start an insurrection "with the vanguard alone."[26] Unfortunately this argument was defective insofar as it was a matter of opinion whether the masses were ready for revolution or not. The statement that it was too early for revolution was always open to challenge by those who took a more sanguine view of the situation.

Yet the Chilean party leadership at first did not appear to appreciate the importance of the new Soviet doctrine of the Peaceful Road. In his report to the Tenth (clandestine) Congress of the Chilean Communists in April 1956 Secretary-General Galo González almost shrugged it off as a mere confirmation of what his own party had been practicing for the last twenty years:

[26] See, for instance, the memorial volume, *Ricardo Fonseca, op. cit.*, p. 166.

The possibility of peaceful revolutionary transition in Chile has not been planted by the congress of the Communist Party of the Soviet Union but by the new international situation prevailing in the world and by our conditions and national characteristics. I have already said that this possibility was demonstrated in Chile by the triumph of the Popular Front in 1938 and the Democratic Alliance in 1946. The experience of other countries has also demonstrated it to a greater degree. And Comrade Khrushchev has done nothing else — a great thing, it is true — but put forward a new thesis in accordance with life, with the practical experience of numerous countries.[27]

And later that year, in an article in the ideological review *Principios,* Galo González seemed mainly concerned with dispelling the impression that the new thesis was revisionist:

As regards the transition to socialism by the Peaceful Road, it is necessary to insist once more that in planting this thesis the Soviet Communist Party did not for one moment mean that the transformations that are necessary for socialism, or, before this, for a regime and program of national liberation, could be of reformist and not of revolutionary character.[28]

For the next four years there was little mention of the Peaceful Road in party documents. For much of this time the Chilean Communists were engaged in fighting the Yugoslav revisionism that was rampant among their Socialist allies. This alone precluded any stress on such a suspicious doctrine as the Peaceful Road, which in spite of Galo González' assurances definitely smacked of that same revisionism.

[27] *El Partido Comunista de Chile y el movimiento comunista internacional, op. cit.,* p. 14.
[28] *Principios,* October 1956.

It was only in 1960 — a momentous year for the international communist movement in general and for the Latin American communists in particular — that the Peaceful Road suddenly became an issue of vital importance for the Chilean Communists.

This was the year in which the Sino-Soviet conflict first became the subject of official debate in the communist world movement. The Chilean Communists had hitherto maintained extremely friendly relations with Peking, and Chilean party intellectuals were employed by the Chinese Communist government as language teachers and lecturers on Latin American literature.[29] Early in 1959, when relations between the Soviet Union and China were already strained, Secretary-General Luis Corvalán[30] went to China, and on his return he made enthusiastic statements that he was later obliged to retract. At that time the Chilean party leaders were still able to delude their followers — and probably themselves — into believing that the Sino-Soviet conflict was a minor difference of opinion on foreign policy and of no concern to the communist world movement.

But in the spring of 1960 the Chinese published their first open attack on the ideological innovations of the Twentieth Congress. At the Bucharest meeting of communist party leaders in June of that year the delegations of 38 communist parties of the "capitalist world" were for the first time directly confronted with the dispute. Then came the weird November 1960 meeting of 81 communist parties in Moscow, in which the entire international communist movement sat in judgment over the Soviet Union and Red China. At this meeting com-

[29] See *ibid.*, September–October 1963.
[30] Secretary-General Galo González had died in 1958.

munists from such countries as Switzerland and Martinique had a voice in working out a document that was supposed to be binding for the foreign policies of the two great powers of the communist bloc. This grotesquely unrealistic venture was of course doomed to failure.

One of the points at issue at the Moscow conference of 81 parties was the Peaceful Road to socialism. The Chinese did not deny the abstract possibility of the conquest of power by peaceful means but pointed out that so far it had never happened in practice.[31] They therefore insisted that it was the duty of every communist party to "walk on both legs," that is, to prepare simultaneously for both a peaceful takeover and the armed struggle.

Through a development originally not connected with the Sino-Soviet dispute at all, the problem of the Peaceful Road had already become crucial for the communist parties of Latin America in general and of Chile in particular. This development was the rapid radicalization of the Cuban revolutionary regime.

In the early stages of the Cuban rising[32] the Chilean Communists, banking on information received from their Cuban brother party, were inclined to regard Fidel Castro and his guerrillas as mere adventurers.[33] By the second half of 1958 they took a somewhat more serious view of the Cuban situation. In his report to the

[31] See the José González report on the Moscow conference of the 81 parties in *El Partido Comunista de Chile y el movimiento comunista internacional*, *op. cit.*, p. 141.

[32] Castro landed in Oriente province on December 2, 1956, and the Batista regime collapsed on December 31, 1958.

[33] See Socialist Secretary-General Raúl Ampuero's taunts in *La polémica socialista-comunista*, published by the party's Central Committee (Santiago de Chile: Prensa Latinoamericana, S. A. [1962]), p. 16.

Eleventh Congress of the Chilean Communists, held in November 1958, Secretary-General Luis Corvalán, after mentioning the successes of the Communist parties of Venezuela, Bolivia, Colombia, Argentina, Brazil, and Honduras, somewhat grudgingly acknowledged that "the struggle of the Cuban people against the sanguinary tyranny of Batista is acquiring greater scope and depth."[34] This was less than two months before Fidel Castro's triumphant entry into Havana. It is significant that the Cuban Communist Party's message to the Chilean Eleventh Congress, signed by Blas Roca and Juan Marinello and dated November 1958, still deplored the "disunity of the opposition forces" and called for "national unity" in order to overthrow the tyranny and form a "democratic coalition government."[35]

Castro's victory made him a popular hero in all of Latin America, and the fact that he subsequently sought and obtained the support of the Soviet Union in his struggle against the United States greatly benefited the Chilean Communists. The Cuban example also produced a radicalization of FRAP policies. FRAP had contested the 1958 election on a moderate platform, and after the election the Eleventh Party Congress stressed the desire to reach agreement "between the political forces of the Left and the Center" for certain basic — again very moderate — immediate aims.[36] But already in March 1960 the Communist Politburo member Orlando Millas, in a report to a Central Committee

[34] See Partido Comunista de Chile, *Documentos del XI Congreso Nacional realizado en noviembre de 1958* (Santiago de Chile: Talleres Gráficos Lautaro, 1959), p. 43.

[35] *Ibid.*, pp. 28 f.

[36] *Ibid.*, p. 129.

session, harshly criticized the "Center parties," that is, the Radicals and the Christian Democrats, and set new, more radical conditions for an understanding with them. These included such demands as "a foreign policy in favor of peace and disarmament," economic links with the Soviet bloc, nationalization of monopoly enterprises, and agrarian reform.[37] Some of these points were certainly not acceptable to the non-Marxist left-of-center parties. Thus the euphoria produced by the Cuban revolution had induced the Chilean Communists to abandon the strategy of broad alliances with limited aims that they had practiced, or attempted to practice, for almost twenty-five years.

But that same year Fidel Castro began to claim for himself the leadership of the Latin American revolutionary movement. This the Chilean Communists could not accept.

Early in 1960 Fidel Castro's henchman "Che" Guevara, the only ideologist that the Castro movement has produced, had published his book, *Guerrilla Warfare*.[38] The main thesis of this book ran counter to two tenets of Leninism on which the communist parties of Latin America had hitherto based their entire activities: first, that a revolution can be successful only if "the objective conditions for it are ripe," and second, that the revolution must be carried out by the urban proletariat, the masses of organized workers. For Guevara proclaimed that "it is not necessary to wait until all conditions for making revolution exist; the insurrection

[37] *El Partido Comunista de Chile y el movimiento comunista internacional, op. cit.,* p. 119.

[38] Ernesto "Che" Guevara, *La guerra de guerrillas;* quotations are from English edition, *Guerrilla Warfare* (New York: Monthly Review Press, 1961).

can create them." In a thinly veiled attack on the communist parties he then railed against "the defeatist attitude of revolutionaries or pseudo-revolutionaries who remain inactive and take refuge in the pretext that against a professional army nothing can be done, who sit down to wait until in some mechanical way all necessary objective and subjective conditions are given without working to accelerate them."[39]

Continuing his attack on communist doctrine, Guevara inveighed against

those who maintain dogmatically that the struggle of the masses is centered in city movements, entirely forgetting the immense participation of the country people in the life of all the underdeveloped parts of America. Of course the struggle of the city masses of organized workers should not be underrated; but their real possibilities of engaging in armed struggle must be carefully analyzed where the guarantees which customarily adorn our constitutions are suspended or ignored. In these conditions the illegal workers' movements face enormous dangers. They must function secretly without arms. The situation in the open country is not so difficult.[40]

It is true that at that time Guevara did not include democratic countries like Chile among those in which a revolution could be induced by guerrilla bands. He specifically stated:

Where a government has come into power through some form of popular vote, fraudulent or not, and maintains at least an appearance of constitutional legality, the guerrilla outbreak cannot be promoted, since the possibilities of peaceful struggle have not yet been exhausted.[41]

[39] *Ibid.*, p. 15.
[40] *Ibid.*, p. 16.
[41] *Ibid.*

Yet this did not prevent the Cuban doctrine of the Violent Road to power from winning adherents in Chile. In the summer of 1960 the president of the Chilean Trade Union Confederation (CUT — Central Unica de Trabajadores de Chile), Clotario Blest, was invited to Cuba. Hitherto a docile fellow traveler of the Communists,[42] he came back a Castroite and fervent advocate of immediate Violent Revolution. Blest did not accept Guevara's doctrine in its literal sense. He believed that in Chile, where the urban working class is far more militant than the peasants, revolution should begin in the city, and that by using his position as leader of the labor unions he would actually be able to set the revolutionary process in motion.

In two inflammatory speeches in November 1960 Blest called upon the Chilean workers to prove that they were capable of having their "own Sierra Maestra," and he announced that "in this country Santiago will be the Sierra Maestra that will smash the reactionaries."[43] Both speeches led to rioting that the Communist and Socialist trade-union officials, who had not been consulted by Blest, had great difficulty in calming down.

This happened in the same month of November in which the 81 communist parties met in Moscow to discuss the Sino-Soviet dispute. The Chilean delegation, led by Assistant Secretary-General José González, sided

[42] Alexander, *Communism in Latin America, op. cit.*, p. 208.

[43] See Luis Vitale, *Los discursos de Clotario Blest y la revolución chilena* (Santiago de Chile: Editorial POR, 1961), pp. 10 and 15. In his speech at the July 26, 1960 celebration in Oriente province, Fidel Castro had coined the slogan that "the Andes mountain range shall be the Sierra Maestra of South America." The Sierra Maestra range in Oriente province, Cuba, had been Castro's mountain stronghold in his two-year guerrilla war against Batista.

with the Soviets. On his return José González gave a detailed report on the Moscow conference to a secret session of the party's Central Committee, extracts from which were published in February 1964.[44]

These highly revealing extracts demonstrate quite clearly that as early as December 1960 the Chilean party leadership was almost as worried about the Cuban heresy as about the Sino-Soviet conflict.

In his report González firmly rejected the Chinese thesis that each party was simultaneously to prepare for peaceful transition and armed struggle:

> The point is that we Communists will take the road that best suits the specific conditions of each country. But in speaking of the two possibilities we are not proposing a dual strategy, that is, that we should prepare for both possibilities. I repeat, we are preparing for that which suits us best, i.e., the peaceful road, and if this road is closed to us and the nonpeaceful road presents itself, we shall not hesitate to take up the armed struggle — always provided that the masses are resolved to take this road to power. . . .
>
> Speaking of the unpeaceful road, in many countries guerrilla bands have been formed, but these will be effective only when the conditions for them exist in a specific country; when there is general discontent, as in the case of Cuba; when in the interior, in the cities, there is a great movement of masses.
>
> In other cases they are not effective. Thus in the case of Spain, as Comrade Dolores[45] pointed out, the guerrillas lasted ten years, the heroism of the Communist guerrilla fighters won applause, but they did not enjoy the support of the people. Thus the party lost its ties with the masses. When the policy was changed, when the party linked up

---

[44] *El Partido Comunista de Chile y el movimiento comunista internacional, op. cit.,* pp. 136–150.

[45] Dolores Ibárruri, *La Pasionaria,* a Spanish Communist leader.

with the masses, when the Communists started to work in the labor unions and to occupy highly responsible posts in them, a wide anti-Franco movement was established.

In Colombia there have also been guerrillas; there have been guerrillas in Burma, in Malaya, but they have sacrificed much and have not reached their goal. In Paraguay the guerrilla movement that managed to fight important battles against Stroessner's army fought in isolation, without links or coordination with the urban workers, which was the cause of its rapid defeat. Now the guerrillas are reorganizing and trying to link their struggle with that of the workers in the factories.[46]

Summing up the attitude of the Chilean party toward the problem of the Peaceful Road, González said:

Our party will continue to fight for the development of the revolutionary struggle by the peaceful road as long as conditions offer us this possibility. We shall fight against all opportunistic and adventurous tendencies of desperate elements and Trotskyist trends in the people's movement. To show the masses an extremist road is easier, but a mistake in the forward march of the revolution, a defeat in the struggle, would retard this forward march for a prolonged period. Irresponsible elements lacking faith in the masses like very much to talk of the armed struggle and of the guerrillas and even try to take the Cuban experience and apply it mechanically to Chile in circumstances where conditions in Cuba were very different. And we may say that if these conditions presented themselves in our country, we would not hesitate for a moment to take advantage of them. Those elements, however, do nothing to create the conditions, to open the road for the forward march of the revolution.

In our country the experience of the workers' and people's movement confirms the possibility of the peaceful development of the revolution. . . .[47]

[46] *El Partido Comunista de Chile y el movimiento comunista internacional, op. cit.*, pp. 141 ff.
[47] *Ibid.*, pp. 148 f.

The González report made it clear that the Moscow conference had failed to close the breach between the Soviet Union and China. But this report remained secret until 1964, and in their public propaganda the Chilean Communists kept asserting that the conference had demonstrated the unity of the entire communist movement and that the talk about Sino-Soviet differences was malicious gossip spread by the capitalist press.

The Chilean Communist propaganda machine also continued to whip up enthusiasm for Cuba. Yet at the same time the polemic against the Sino-Cuban thesis of Violent Revolution was continued, albeit in such form that the general public, and probably also the bulk of the ordinary party members, remained unaware of its real significance.

In January 1961, two months after the Moscow meeting, Secretary-General Luis Corvalán published an article on the Peaceful Road in the party's ideological review. In this article he again stressed what had now become a crucial point for the party leaders: that the party did not intend to pursue a dual policy of preparing both for a peaceful take-over and an armed struggle:

On the basis of the fact that revolution by the peaceful road does not depend solely on a decision by the proletariat, some people maintain that it is necessary to prepare for the alternative of the violent road at the same time. This is correct in general terms, and it primarily requires a communist party to be sufficiently alert to appreciate changes in the situation that call for a change in tactics. But preparation for the violent alternative where there is the possibility of the peaceful road does not consist in such undertakings as already forming armed detachments. In practice this would mean a double line, marching simultaneously by both roads, with the consequent dispersion of forces, and it would expose the people's movement, or part of it, to adventure, to provocative coups, to a leftist and sectarian line. Moreover, the experience of all violent revolutions has demonstrated that the problem of arms is not insolvable; it solves itself on a grand scale at the appropriate moment by the action of the masses, who overcome the enemy forces and draw part of them over into the trenches of the revolution.[48]

In the same article Corvalán stated:

The great transformations now taking place in Cuba will have to come about in all of Latin America, but not necessarily by the same road in all of our countries. In the majority of them the revolution will perhaps take the Violent Road. But in Chile we insist that we consider the Peaceful Road to be viable. In any case, there is nothing more pernicious for the people's movement than mechanically trying to copy the revolutionary processes that are taking place or will take place in other places. As Lenin said: "All countries will reach socialism; this is inevitable, but they will not reach it in the same manner. . . ."

After the annihilation of the Bay of Pigs landing party the Chilean Communists' enthusiasm for Castro and their campaign for solidarity with Cuba reached new heights. But this did not prevent them from teaming up with their Socialist allies to eliminate the Chilean Castroite Clotario Blest from the leadership of the Trade Union Confederation. Blest's position now became untenable, his small band of Trotskyist, anarchist, and left-wing Socialist supporters being outnumbered by a compact Socialist-Communist majority.

In August 1961, on the eve of the Third Congress

---

[48] *Principios*, January–February 1961.

of the Chilean Trade Union Confederation, Luis Corvalán made the following statement aimed at Blest:

There are some people with responsible posts in the
workers' and people's movement who jump as if their corns
had been trodden on every time that we Communists alert
the people against the adventurers and provocateurs who
have the audacity to present us as engaged in doing a
"fire-brigade's job" in the workers' movement. And as for
their charges that we are braking the class struggle, these
do not bother us. The workers know us, and this is enough.
We shall not join anyone in a marathon of ultrarevolu-
tionary verbiage, and much less in wild actions. We do
not need to play at revolution and Sierra Maestra in order
to affirm ourselves as revolutionaries.[49]

At the congress itself Blest resigned from the presidency of the Confederation. When the white-haired
old man stood up to defend his policies, a horde of
Communist-inspired teen-age thugs in the galleries
shouted him down, and to indicate that by his alliance
with the Trotskyists he had sold out to the enemies of
the working class, a shower of low-denomination coins
descended on his bowed head.[50]

This scene took place only a few weeks after Fidel
Castro in his speech at the July 26 celebrations in
Havana had announced the amalgamation of his own
movement with the Cuban Communists as a decisive
step toward the formation of a unified Marxist-Leninist
party and therefore also toward the transformation of
the Cuban regime from a personal dictatorship into a
communist party dictatorship of the orthodox type.

[49] *El Partido Comunista de Chile y el movimiento comunista internacional, op. cit.,* pp. 152 f.
[50] See the article by Tito Stefoni in the review *Polémica,* No. 11,
1964.

This development made it necessary for the Chilean party to explain that it was not waging an ideological struggle against the Castroite Clotario Blest but had removed him from the leadership of the labor movement purely and simply because he was an "adventurer." Luis Corvalán undertook this difficult task in a second article on the Peaceful Road, which appeared in the October 1961 issue of *Principios* and in which he greatly modified what he had written in his first article nine months before.

Thus Corvalán now stressed that the Peaceful Road did not necessarily mean victory in an election. He defined this road as

the road of the struggle of the masses, who may, at a certain point, even seize power without elections, utilizing other channels, other forms of action, other possibilities. . . . The important thing is to grasp that the concept of the Peaceful Road includes diverse situations that may occur and various forms of mass struggle, including acute forms of the class struggle, such as the general strike, and excluding the use of violence only in the form of civil war or the armed insurrection of the entire people.

Corvalán even backtracked to a certain extent on his previous statement that the party was against a dual policy of simultaneous preparation for a peaceful takeover and an armed struggle:

In a previous article (*Principios*, No. 77, January 1961) we said that "preparation for the violent alternative where there is the possibility of the Peaceful Road does not consist in such undertakings as *already* forming armed detachments." With the word "already," which we now underline, we do not discard the possibility that, at a certain moment, even the formation of such detachments will be undertaken. For instance, in case the reactionaries carry out their intention of forming White Guards against the people, it will be necessary to constitute a people's militia. . . .

Corvalán repeated his warning that one must not mechanically apply the Cuban experience to the other countries of Latin America. But this warning now had an entirely different meaning:

One may say that in our country, in case the revolution definitely took a violent course, the most probable development would be that this would not happen as in Cuba, that is, with a guerrilla center in the countryside, which in the course of nearly three years smashed the regular army. . . . In Chile violent revolution would perhaps start in the cities, would express itself in a rising of the proletariat with a combination of general or partial strikes and street fighting, and, naturally, with the support of the masses of the countryside, and it would only last for a few days or weeks at the most. This is the conclusion that may be reached by taking into account the class-struggle traditions of the Chilean working class, the circumstance that no government could hold out for a month against a strike paralyzing the main economic activities . . . and that, unlike the situation that prevailed in Cuba, where the labor movement was controlled by Batista agents, here it is in the hands of the workers themselves. These observations do not imply for a moment that we underestimate the possibilities of the struggle in the countryside and of the peasantry as the indispensable ally of the proletariat.

Corvalán then stretched out his hand to all serious proponents of the Violent Road, rejecting only "adventurers" such as Clotario Blest and his friends:

Whatever the definite road of the Chilean revolution . . . it is fundamental to understand that the essential tasks of the present day are the same in either case: to push forward and lead the struggle of the masses, to strengthen and develop the unity and combativeness of the working class, to strengthen even more the workers' and peasants' alliance, to work for the rallying of the majority of the Chilean nation around the proletariat. . . .

Since this is so, there is no reason whatsoever why, in virtue of our thesis of the peaceful road, there should arise discrepancies with those who, without believing in the peaceful road, sincerely fight for the revolution. The discrepancies arise with those who want to replace the tasks of the moment, the real revolutionary tasks, by adventurous activities that have nothing to do with the thesis of the violent road.

Lately in our country Trotskyist and anarchist elements, and other elements under their influence, such as the ex-president of CUT, Clotario Blest, have tried to pose as the partisans of the violent road. But every worker of any experience and everyone with even a rudimentary knowledge of the teachings of Marxism-Leninism on the subject of revolution will inevitably reach the conclusion that such people and their designs are completely irresponsible. In whatever form, the struggle for revolution is a mass struggle and has nothing to do with adventurism, with a propensity for coups, with desperate cries for "direct action," and with attempts to deny the vanguard role of the party of the working class. . . .

One may doubt that this article denoted a genuine change of heart on the part of the Chilean party leadership, but it was certainly a major effort to come to terms with the Cubans, to demonstrate that such differences of opinion as existed were not vital, and thus to shelve the issue of the Peaceful Road.

This attempt can be understood only in the context of the international situation prevailing in September and October 1961. At that time Fidel Castro appeared to be willing to leave the leadership of the new party and hence of the Cuban state in the hands of the old-guard Communists, most of whom were dependable followers of Moscow. From the Soviet and Chilean Communist point of view the situation thus appeared to be under control. Furthermore the Soviet Union seemed to be definitely embarked on a policy of expansion in Latin America, and this bolstered the self-confidence of the Chilean Communists and their belief in an early victory — either by peaceful or by not-quite-so-peaceful means. This made the differences of opinion with the Castroites seem unimportant. The debate thus calmed down when there appeared to be a real prospect of victory for the revolution — only to start again and become more heated than ever a year later, when this prospect faded as a result of the Caribbean crisis.

Meanwhile the wider issue of the Sino-Soviet conflict came to the fore again. At the Twenty-Second Congress of the Soviet Communists in that same October 1961, Khrushchev's open attack on China's ally Albania produced what may in retrospect be regarded as the definite rupture between China and the Soviet Union. At the same congress the attacks on Stalin and on the "antiparty group" were surprisingly resumed. The dismay that these events caused in the communist world movement was perhaps as great as that caused by the Twentieth Congress, but the authority of the Soviet leadership was by then greater than it had been in 1956, having been considerably strengthened by the Soviet successes in rocketry and the exploration of space and by the Soviet Union's apparent military ascendency over the United States. The Chilean Communists displayed better discipline than on the previous occasion, when their Secretary-General had displayed such lack of enthusiasm in commenting on Khrushchev's ideological innovation of the Peaceful Road.

At the Soviet party congress itself the Chilean guest delegate, Secretary-General Luis Corvalán, condemned the attitude of the Albanians toward the Soviet party and expressed the hope that the Albanians would return to the fold.[51] Later, in his report to the Chilean Central Committee, Corvalán stated that the Albanians had "resorted to the same anti-Leninist methods that Stalin had applied in the leadership of the party and the state." He specifically mentioned the tragic case of the female member of the Albanian Politburo, Liri Gega, who "was sentenced to death together with her husband, and in a condition when she was most worthy of respect, when about to become a mother."[52] In the same report Corvalán emphatically pronounced himself against polycentrism: "The recognition or acceptance of this principle would lead to nationalism, to dispersion and ideological confusion, and to the weakening of the unity of the communists. . . ."[53] He made an impressive profession of loyalty to the Soviet Union:

. . . Since its beginnings the communist movement has been essentially internationalist, and it has always had a directing center in the best sense of the word, in the sense of a vanguard of advanced ideas.

It is clear that the center of the international communist movement cannot be situated in Santiago de Chile or in Tirana, in London or in Peking, or in any part of the world other than the Soviet Union.

This center has already been situated there for a long time, not by a unilateral decision of the Soviet party, nor even by an accord of all the parties, but in virtue of a con-

[51] *El Partido Comunista de Chile y el movimiento comunista internacional, op. cit.,* p. 170.
[52] *Ibid.,* p. 188.
[53] *Ibid.,* p. 191.

juncture of historical circumstances that all of them have understood and recognized.[54]

As for the Chinese, Corvalán stated:

The Communist Party of Chile has maintained cordial relations with the Communist Party of China and hopes to continue to do so. But we cannot refrain from expressing our preoccupation in view of what has happened.

There are some people who ask whether some schism is threatening the international communist movement.

We are not prophets . . . but we are convinced that what is actually in process is the formation of the most solid unity of principle of the international communist movement. . . .[55]

On February 8, 1961 the Chilean Central Committee sent a letter to the Chinese party, brief extracts of which have only recently been published. In this letter the Chileans stressed that

In Chile the reactionary press, the Trotskyist groups, and other enemies of the workers' movement wage a sustained campaign of scandal and misinterpretation based on the positions maintained by the Communist Party of China. Furthermore the position of your party concerning the problem of peaceful coexistence has been joyfully welcomed by the Trotskyists and other renegades of the revolutionary movement.[56]

In March 1962 the Communist Party of Chile staged its Twelfth National Congress. It is indicative of the status the Chilean Communists enjoy in the political life of their country that they were allowed to hold the opening session of their congress in the ceremonial hall of the Chilean parliament building.

[54] *Ibid.*, p. 189.
[55] *Ibid.*, pp. 192 f.
[56] *Ibid.*, p. 206.

Secretary-General Luis Corvalán's keynote speech reflected boundless enthusiasm for Cuba and a firm conviction that the day of victory in Chile was near. He said that "the glorious Cuban revolution . . . marks the beginning of a new phase in Latin America's struggle for its full independence, for progress, democracy, and socialism."[57] According to him "the triumphant march of our peoples on the road to independence is irresistible. The wonderful example of Cuba inspires them."[58]

Although he certainly knew better, Corvalán maintained that the Moscow Declaration of the 81 parties had "demonstrated the unity of ideas and action of the communists of the entire world."[59] He condemned the Albanians, who had "fallen into the mire of anti-Sovietism."[60] He also insisted that

the shortest road to the construction of socialism is certainly not through war but through the triumph of peaceful co-existence, peace, and disarmament. . . . In conditions of peaceful coexistence the struggle of the peoples for their independence is made easier. In such conditions it is more difficult for the imperialist powers to interfere in the internal affairs of other countries. . . .[61]

On the other hand, Corvalán's brief reference to the Peaceful Road was definitely equivocal:

The working class and the people, who wish to come to power without an armed struggle, have to keep in mind the possibility that the enemy will incite one. That is why

[57] *Hacia la conquista de un gobierno popular: documentos del XII Congreso Nacional del Partido Comunista de Chile* (Santiago de Chile: Soc. Impresora "Horizonte," 1962), p. 12.

[58] *Ibid.*, p. 29.

[59] *Ibid.*, p. 14.

[60] *Ibid.*, p. 66.

[61] *Ibid.*, p. 22.

they have to prepare for any eventuality. The measures to
be taken to that end will have to be determined by the
people's organizations themselves. What is important is
that they be taken. . . .[62]

It was left to another member of the Politburo,
Orlando Millas, to make clear to the party cadres that
the party leadership still rejected a dual policy of preparing for both a peaceful takeover and an armed
struggle. In his speech to the congress Millas declared:

There are some people on the Left who, under pretext
of the undisputable need to prepare for every eventuality,
engage in conjecture and idle speculation on the violent
road, presenting it as another, immediate alternative. This
position is dangerous in diverting the attention of the
people's forces from the real objective, which consists in
directing the maximum effort, concentrating the interest of
the majority of the nation on the preservation of civil liberties, on resistance to any attempt at repression, on guaran-
teeing democratic rights, and on demanding and obtaining
respect for the country's determination to give itself an
anti-imperialist government. There is talk of a policy of
the "two legs," of moving at the same time along two lines,
one the peaceful road and the other the violent road.
We hold the theory of two lines, two different legs, to be
pernicious because it makes you limp, and we prefer to
walk with two equal legs that belong to one sole Marxist-
Leninist body."[63]

At the time of their Twelfth Party Congress the
Chilean Communists had every reason to believe that
their Cuban brother party was firmly entrenched in
power. Communist Party stalwarts were in charge of
the organization and the indoctrination of the new
Marxist-Leninist party that was then in process of

[62] *Ibid.*, p. 56.
[63] *Ibid.*, p. 154.

formation. One of them, Aníbal Escalante, controlled the party machine. Many of Fidel Castro's non-Communist friends from the days of the guerrilla war had been eliminated, and Castro himself appeared to be destined to become a mere figurehead, with reliable Moscovite Communists actually running the government. In consequence, relations between the Cuban revolutionary government and the Chilean and other Latin American communist parties were extremely cordial.

Then, only a few days after the Chilean party congress had ended, events in Cuba took a surprising turn. In a dramatic coup Castro removed Escalante from his post and took over control of the party machine himself. He made a television speech denouncing the old-guard Communists for their "sectarianism" and "dogmatism" and for their policy of discriminations against the heroes of the guerrilla war. Very soon a number of the non-Communist veterans began drifting back into positions of influence.

What had actually happened was that after letting the old-guard Communists build the skeleton of the new ruling party Castro assumed command himself. As the undisputed leader of a Marxist-Leninist party, the only such party in power in the Western Hemisphere, he was now in a better position than ever to claim the leadership of the Latin American revolutionary Left and to press his policy of Violent Revolution on other communist parties. After some hesitation the Soviets accepted the new situation, and *Pravda* published an editorial applauding Castro and censuring the "sectarianism" of the old and trusted Soviet agent Escalante. But in reality Moscow played a double game. The same *Pravda* editorial stated plainly that the new Cuban ruling party now controlled by Castro was not yet a true Marxist-Leninist party but only on its way to becoming one. This was clearly a signal to the Latin American communists not to accept Castro's leadership role.

As a result, relations between the Chilean Communists and the Castro regime deteriorated, and the visits of high Chilean party dignitaries to the island ceased. This development, however, remained unknown to the general public and even to the party's rank and file, since the party's propaganda machine continued to praise Cuba to the skies. And even to the party leaders Cuba remained an example in at least one respect — it appeared to demonstrate the weakness of the United States and to prove that the Soviet Union would be able and willing to protect any other communist regime that might be established in the Western Hemisphere.

Both these assumptions were disproved in the Caribbean crisis of October 1962.

REPERCUSSIONS OF THE CARIBBEAN CRISIS

When Khrushchev announced the Soviet decision to withdraw the rockets from Cuba, the Politburo of the Chilean Communists hailed the action in a public statement as

a great victory for the forces of peace, in preventing the outbreak of war and assuring the integrity of Cuba and its independence, which was threatened by North American imperialism. . . . We Communists consider that this triumph belongs to all those in the entire world who rose up against the Yankee war measures, in the first place to the nations led by the Soviet people. . . . Latin America has won a political battle of incalculable consequences. . . .

. . . The fact that President Kennedy's offer to commit himself to respect the integrity of Cuba was immediately followed by the Soviet agreement to withdraw the weapons to which the North Americans had objected demonstrates that these arms were not there for any offensive purpose. . . . It is a lie that the full independence of Cuba was in any way impaired. . . .[64]

But this was mere braggadocio. The plain facts were that the United States had forced a showdown and that the Soviet Union had backed out. This disproved the assumptions on which Soviet foreign policy had been based for several years, that is, ever since the intercontinental ballistic missile had been put into service by the Soviet army. The Soviets had evidently come to assume that the United States was morally, if not materially, so weak that in a showdown it would prefer ignominious retreat to the risk of war. This assumption had apparently been corroborated by the fact that the United States had allowed the Soviets to install themselves in Cuba during 1960–1962 and had refrained from using even its air force to back up the Bay of Pigs landing in April 1961.

The Caribbean crisis showed that this tolerance of the Soviet presence in Cuba was not due to moral weakness but to a mere underestimation of Soviet aggressiveness on the part of the United States government. Washington had simply not believed that the Soviets would dare to use the island as a military base. As long as no such base was established, the Castro regime, irksome though it might be, did not constitute enough of a threat to the

[64] *El Partido Comunista de Chile y el movimiento comunista internacional, op. cit.,* p. 224.

security of the United States to warrant direct military action. But as soon as the threat materialized, the United States acted rapidly and effectively.

The discovery that the United States would fight if seriously threatened forced the Soviet leaders to a re-orientation of their foreign policy. What they now needed was a breathing space, at least until their scientists had invented some superweapon that would give them an overwhelming advantage over the United States.

Two courses lay open to the Soviet leaders in order to obtain this breathing space. They could either retrench, withdraw from exposed positions such as Cuba, and return to the policy of sullen isolation and inactivity practiced by Molotov in the years immediately following Stalin's death, or they could make some slight propitiatory gestures such as a revival of disarmament talks and the expansion of trade with the West. The latter would probably suffice to reduce world tension and to slacken the pace of the armament race. It might even obviate the necessity for a Soviet strategic withdrawal from advanced positions, thus enabling the Soviet Union to maintain its foothold in the Western Hemisphere. But further expansion appeared for the time being to be out of the question.

Judging by subsequent developments, the Soviets chose this second course as the lesser evil, although even a slight and superficial rapprochement with the United States was bound further to increase Sino-Soviet tension.

The reorientation of Soviet foreign policy had far-reaching effects on the strategy of the Latin American communist parties. It now appeared probable that if one of these parties came to power, by whatever means, the United States would regard such a development as a threat to its vital interests and would take measures against Soviet support of the new regime. There would be another showdown on the Cuban pattern — exactly what the Soviets now wanted to avoid. As long as they were interested in achieving at least a temporary détente in their relations with the United States, they could not desire further trouble in Latin America.

How did the communist parties of Latin America react to this new situation? One of them, the Communist Party of Venezuela, escaped from Soviet tutelage[65] in order to continue with its policy of immediate Violent Revolution. But other parties returned to the time-honored policy of broad alliances with limited aims. Thus in the June 1963 election the Peruvian Communists supported the left-of-center moderate Belaúnde Terry, and since his victory they have continued to collaborate with him.[66] In Argentina the Communists had formed an alliance with the violently anti-American, pro-Cuban left wing of the Peronista movement and supported Perón's call for a blank vote in the July 1963 presidential election; but when the moderate Radical, Illía, was elected, the Communists broke away from the Peronistas and adopted a policy of qualified support for the new president. It is to be noted that both Illía and Belaúnde cooperate with the Alliance for Progress,

[65] At the East German party congress in January 1963, the Venezuelan party was absent from the list of Latin American parties that supported the Chilean delegate in his condemnation of Albania.
[66] This moderate policy of the Peruvian party leadership has since led to a split in the Peruvian party; in January 1964 a pro-Chinese group called a "national conference" that formally "expelled" the old-guard Acosta–Del Prado leadership.

although Belaúnde has expressed doubts as to its efficacy. The Alliance for Progress had hitherto been one of the main targets of Communist vituperation, and a year earlier it would have been unthinkable for the Communists to support any government that did not reject the Alliance.

In a report published in the Chilean Communist Party newspaper *El Siglo* on July 18, 1963, Politburo member Orlando Millas expressed a favorable opinion of both Belaúnde and Illía, thus indicating Chilean party support for the policies of the Peruvian and Argentinian brother parties. In their own country, however, the Chilean Communists were not free to return to their old policy of broad alliances with limited aims.

In December 1962, less than two months after the Caribbean crisis, the Chilean Socialists had formally announced the candidacy of Senator Salvador Allende for the presidential election of September 1964. In January 1963 the Communists followed suit by announcing their support of Allende.

This action precluded a broad alliance with either of the two important non-Marxist left-of-center groups. Neither the Radicals nor the Christian Democrats could accept Allende or any other Socialist or Communist as their candidate since each of the two Marxist parties was considerably smaller than their own.[67] The only possibility for a broad alliance with the Radicals or the Christian Democrats would have been for the Socialists and Communists to waive their claim to a candidate of their own. This the Socialists refused to do, and the Communists could not afford to lose their only sure ally

[67] 1963 municipal elections: Christian Democrats — 452,000 votes; Radicals — 427,000; Communists — 254,000; Socialists — 230,000.

in the mere hope of being able to come to terms with one of the big non-Marxist parties. Since their own followers would not have understood such a move, they were forced to go along with the Socialists and keep to their previous policy of a narrow proletarian alliance.

Some weeks later the Communists' discomforture was increased by the reappearance of their old enemy, former President Gabriel González Videla, on the political scene. González Videla successfully promoted the nomination of his friend and protégé Senator Julio Durán as the presidential candidate first of the Radical Party and then of the entire government coalition of Radicals, Liberals, and Conservatives. Since this coalition obtained nearly 45 per cent of the total vote in the 1963 municipal elections, Durán appeared to have an excellent chance of winning the presidency in 1964. In that event the Communists could no longer expect the same impartial treatment at the hands of the government that they currently enjoyed under President Jorge Alessandri.

President Alessandri was a man of rigidly conservative opinions who could not be accused of sympathies for Marxism or any tendency toward political flirtation with the Communists. But he was careful not to discriminate against them. He did not fail to call their parliamentary leaders in for briefings together with those of the other opposition parties. He appeared to regard anticommunist rhetoric as beneath his dignity and rarely replied to their tirades against his government, preferring to direct his ire against the more moderate Christian Democratic opposition.

The Communists visibly appreciated this treatment. Although they were unsparing in their criticism of his policies, their polemics against him were free from the vituperation and personal denigration that they heaped on certain other political figures, notably ex-President González Videla and Senator Julio Durán.

If Julio Durán became president, he might well promote repressive measures against the Communists and, if they resisted, revive his sponsor González Videla's Law for the Defense of Democracy. On the other hand, although the Christian Democratic candidate Eduardo Frei was certainly not pro-Communist, they could expect from him the same impartial treatment as from Alessandri.[68] Furthermore, since he was a left-of-center reformer, it would not be in his interest as president to weaken the Left by repressive measures, because this would make him dependent on the parliamentary support of the conservative right-of-center parties opposed to his program of reform.

Considering the circumstances, it would have been advantageous for the Communists to support the Christian Democratic candidate. Since their alliance with the Socialists made this impossible, they at least tried not overduly to antagonize the Christian Democrats, toning down their polemics against them and avoiding personal attacks on Frei, while concentrating their fire on Durán. Furthermore they did their best to keep the election campaign as quiet and orderly as possible in order not to provoke repressive measures and perhaps even more in order not to stampede the middle-class electorate, a large sector of which was in favor of Frei, into the camp of the militantly anti-Communist Durán. In short, the Communists' policy was a defensive one,

[68] In 1948, Frei and his Falange Nacional voted against the law banning the Communist Party.

the sober policy of sober men who were thinking of the possibility of defeat as well as of victory and were unwilling to burn the boats that they might later need for a retreat.

Their Socialist allies, on the other hand, consistently stressed that Frei, not Durán, was the main enemy and obstacle on FRAP's road to victory. Events after the government coalition's defeat by a FRAP candidate in the Curicó by-election of March 1964 seemed to prove them right. The Liberals and Conservatives switched their support to Frei, and Durán ceased to be a serious competitor. Only in the last months of the election campaign did the Communists throw all caution to the winds and join the Socialists in an all-out attack on Frei and the Christian Democrats as the representatives of imperialism and monopoly capitalism and as "the other face of the Right."

One of the first visible effects of the Caribbean crisis was the revival of the Peaceful Road controversy. Luis Corvalán himself brought up the issue, which one year earlier he had proposed to shelve. In the December 1962 issue of the ideological review of the international communist movement, *Problems of Peace and Socialism,* which was actually not issued until January 1963, he published an article on "The Struggle for the Formation of a People's Government in Chile." It contained, first, a remarkable tribute to the democratic traditions of the Chilean nation, which, according to Corvalán, would make it difficult for an anticommunist coup d'état to succeed:

At present the main danger in Chile is that of an ultra-reactionary coup. The struggle against this danger is the first duty of the revolutionaries. But it must be pointed out that the coup d'état aimed at the formation of an unconstitutional government of a fascist type encounters very serious difficulties. The immense majority of the nation is against coups. The government coalition parties themselves devote themselves to exalting what they term representative democracy, presenting Chile as an example of democratic government and constitutional normality. Such sermons find a response in the citizenry so that the ruling classes, if they tried to leave this road, would be left with a precarious social base and faced by mass resistance. In these circumstances this type of coup d'état might even end favorably for the people.

Second, Corvalán very emphatically came out against a dual policy:

In speaking of the possibility of a peaceful solution, one implicitly recognizes that the situation may also engender another alternative, a nonpeaceful, violent alternative, and for this reason it is necessary to be prepared for every eventuality. But the two possibilities cannot be regarded simultaneously and on the same plane as immediate alternatives. This would not only lead to a dual orientation but at the same time, and as a result of the existence of two lines, to political confusion. In our specific case it would also lead to a weakening of the struggle for something so fundamental as the battle [sic] for democratic liberties, against repressive measures, against the danger of a fascist coup.

Third, Corvalán explicitly stated that the Cuban experience did not apply to Chile and lashed out against the Chilean Castroite Clotario Blest:

The fact that in Cuba the revolution came to power by the violent road is sometimes interpreted as signifying that this is the only road for all the countries of the continent. But the matter does not lend itself to simplification. Cuba's great contribution consists, first, in having demonstrated the possibility of breaking with imperialism in Latin

America; second, in having demonstrated the possibility of taking the road of the construction of socialism; and third, in having demonstrated that the triumph of a people's national liberation and, further on, socialist revolution is not necessarily bound up with an international war.

As for the manner of making the revolution, history has vindicated Fidel Castro. Even more, one may safely assume that the road taken over there is also, speaking in general terms, the most probable road in other countries, perhaps in most of the countries of the continent. But there can be no certainty that *all* of them will take this road. Such a certainty would lead to the abandonment of positions already conquered and to the neglect of factual potentialities.

At this stage of the development of events in Chile it may be affirmed that objectively the revolutionary process is taking a peaceful road, the road that, in accordance with reality, our party pointed out. In practice all the parties of the Popular Action Front agree on this point. The adventurers and dogmatists have been pushed aside. This is what happened, for example, to Clotario Blest, ex-President of CUT, who has lately gone over to Trotskyist positions and who did not even manage to get himself re-elected as the leader of the Trade Union Confederation at its last congress.[69]

As was to be expected, the months following the Cuban crisis also brought about a further widening of the Sino-Soviet rift. The Chinese had eagerly supported Fidel Castro in his protests against the manner in which the Soviet Union had backed down during the Cuban crisis.[70] The Soviets, on the other hand, had failed to give moral and political support to the Chinese attack on India. In the months that followed, Chinese guest delegates used the congresses of several East and West

[69] Translated from *Nuestra Epoca*, No. 12, December 1962.
[70] The Chinese criticize Khrushchev not only for withdrawing the rockets but even more for putting them there in the first place.

European communist parties to put China's grievances against the Soviet Union before an international communist forum. The Soviets used the same meetings to demonstrate that the overwhelming majority of the communist parties was on their side. To this purpose they induced the guest delegates to condemn Albania in their speeches; for at this stage of the conflict each side still directed its attacks against the other side's proxy — Yugoslavia in the Chinese, and Albania in the Soviet case.

In every instance the Chilean guest delegate sided with the Soviets. The most significant speech made by a Chilean guest delegate at any of these congresses was that of Politburo member Orlando Millas at the East German party congress in January 1963.

Millas maintained that in the Caribbean crisis Nikita Khrushchev had saved the world from war:

The raising of the blockade of Cuba and the undoing of the invasion prepared by the Pentagon constitute a great triumph for the forces of peace and in particular of the valiant Cuban people.[71]

In an allusion to the Sino-Soviet conflict Millas deplored the attitude of those

who appear to be seeking the division of the communist movement, since they resort to calumnies against the party of Lenin itself, undermine the ideological and organizational principles, and promote the peril of factionalism. As for us, we emphatically condemn the bourgeois nationalist attitudes and repeat our protest against the provocations of the Albanian leaders.[72]

This declaration acquired its particular importance

[71] See *El Siglo*, February 3, 1963.
[72] *Ibid.*

from the fact that Millas spoke not only in the name of the Chilean Communists but also for sixteen other Latin American communist parties, most of whose delegates were present at the congress but had waived their right to speak. The seventeen parties represented by Millas were those of Argentina, Bolivia, Brazil, Colombia, Costa Rica, Chile, Ecuador, Guatemala, Haiti, Honduras, Nicaragua, Panama, Paraguay, Peru, the Dominican Republic, El Salvador, and Uruguay.

It is interesting to note that both Cuba and Venezuela were missing from this list. At previous European party congresses Cuba had been represented by old-guard Communists like Blas Roca, who had dutifully echoed the general condemnation of Albania. But to the East German congress Fidel Castro had delegated his tough henchman Armando Hart, who was not a member of the old Communist Party now fused with Castro's own movement in the United Party of the Socialist Revolution (PURS). In his speech to the congress Hart failed to condemn Albania, thus indicating that Cuba was not on the Soviet side.

CHINESE INTERVENTION

In the course of 1962 such Albanian pamphlets as "Deeper and Deeper into the Mire of Anti-Marxism," a savage attack on Khrushchev, began to arrive in Chile. Later, Chinese polemical articles were also sent to Chile. This caused the Central Committee of the Chilean Communist Party to send a second letter to the Chinese party in January 1963. According to an official summary, made public in February 1964, the letter to the Chinese dealt mainly with "the comportment of this party's representatives at the congresses of the Communist parties of Bulgaria, Hungary, Czechoslovakia, and Italy, as well as the situation created by the Sino-Indian frontier conflict.[73] It then registered the following complaint:

Before terminating this letter we wish to tell the Chinese comrades frankly and openly that we feel preoccupied and justifiably worried by certain situations that affect the normal and fraternal relations between our two parties.

Continually and in increasing quantities, broad mass organizations are receiving a copious correspondence from the Albanian Party of Labor, as well as some Chinese publications, which, instead of furthering the ideological and political unity of the communist movement, insist on accentuating the divergencies to which we have referred above and, what is worse, are threatening to confuse many elements.[74]

This protest was disregarded by the Chinese. Indeed they now greatly stepped up their ideological drive in Chile. On March 6 the first number of *Pekin Informa,* the Spanish-language edition of the fortnightly *Peking Review,* was published. That same month a commercial firm named Espártaco Editores Ltda. (Spartacus Publishers Ltd.) was entered in the Chilean Trade Register. This firm, which shared an office in downtown Santiago with the New China News Agency, handled the distribution of Chinese propaganda materials in Chile and other Latin American countries and also published, significantly, a booklet containing the text of Fidel Castro's speech of February 22, 1963 on the "United Party of the Socialist Revolution." To the chagrin of the

---

[73] *El Partido Comunista de Chile y el movimiento comunista internacional, op. cit.,* p. 227.
[74] *Ibid.,* p. 228.

Communists, two FRAP newspapers, the independent morning tabloid *Clarín* and the Socialist afternoon tabloid *Ultima Hora,* printed advertisements announcing that subscriptions for *Pekin Informa* could be obtained at the Espártaco Editores office.

Espártaco Editores was staffed by a group of Communist Party intellectuals who soon became known as the "Spartacus group." Besides their open activities as publishers and as distributors of Chinese propaganda materials, the Spartacus group was apparently engaged in clandestine factional activities inside the Communist Party, such as distributing the veteran American Communist Anna Louise Strong's Peking newsletter, which was not made available to the general public.[75]

The Chilean Communist Party had hitherto treated the Sino-Soviet dispute as an internal party matter and had refrained from public attacks on the Chinese. The activities of Espártaco Editores now obliged it to change its attitude. In March 1963 the party newspaper *El Siglo* began publishing entire series of articles from the Italian and French Communist press that dealt critically with various aspects of the Chinese ideological platform. Furthermore, on March 30, 1963 the Politburo of the Communist Party of Chile publicly notified the party membership that the Chinese propaganda materials were against the party line:

In response to various inquiries regarding the circulation in our country of ostensibly Marxist-Leninist documents at-

[75] To counteract the impression made by the Anna Louise Strong newsletter, *El Siglo* of July 4, 1963 published a page-long blast stating in effect that Anna Louise Strong lived luxuriously in Peking, "in a beautiful mansion surrounded by gardens, which before the liberation had been the seat of the Italian embassy and which today also lodges the Chinese Peace Committee."

tacking the line of the international communist movement
as well as several brother parties the Politburo declares
that the line of the Communist Party of Chile is incompatible with the contents of these documents. At the same time
it is our duty to recommend to the members of the party
and of the people's movement a deeper study of the Moscow Declarations of the representatives of the communist
and workers' parties of 1957 and 1960, and of the programmatic documents of the Communist Party of Chile, the
Communist Party of the Soviet Union, and of other brother
parties that defend this general orientation.[76]

The answer to this edict came from a most unlikely
quarter: The Central Committee of the Albanian party
addressed a letter to the Chilean Central Committee.
The Spartacus group saw to it that copies of this letter
reached a large number of party activists and later, in
February 1964, even handed it to the Conservative
newspaper *Diario Ilustrado* for publication.

In the characteristic violent style cultivated by the
Albanian polemicists the letter started off with the assertion that

the struggle to restore and safeguard the unity of Marxist-
Leninist principles in the communist and workers' parties
and true proletarian internationalism against the criminal
divisionist and capitulationist activities of the Tito-Khru-
shchev clique of appeasers of imperialism has reached a
new and crucial stage.

The main feature of the Albanian letter was a savage
attack on Luis Corvalán and a denunciation of the international activities of the Chilean party leadership:

We are writing to you because we have become aware,
by our own experience as well as by information that has

[76] *El Partido Comunista de Chile y el movimiento comunista internacional, op. cit.*, pp. 228 f.

reached us, that your party is with almost complete certainty the one in Latin America that is the most exposed to these unprincipled tactics of contemporary revisionism. There have been coarse attempts to put pressure on party members, such as the declaration published in *El Siglo* on March 30, in which truly Leninist materials were condemned in the accustomed manner as "ostensibly Marxist-Leninist," attacking the general line of the international communist movement. That Luis Corvalán accepts the unilateral and subjectivist interpretations of the 81 parties by the contemporary revisionists as the "general line of the movement" — this we already know. Like other contemporary revisionists, he obeys the conductor's baton and declares that unquestioning loyalty to the leaders of the Communist Party of the Soviet Union is the true proof of proletarian internationalism. Does this man really believe, as the Declaration of the 81 parties puts it, that all the parties are truly independent and equal? You know better than anyone that he was in fact one of the first to demand such servility — and to demand it of you — in his report on the 22nd Congress of the Russian CP. To us, his true character was revealed in a glaring light at that same congress, when he attacked and denounced us in the name but without the authority of your party, blindly accepting as true all the lies and calumnies that were at that time circulated by the divisionists. He will be able to live well — the divisionists pay well — but he must be without principles and pride. You know about his activities in his own country, but what about his activity on the international level? Do you realize that from the opening of the Bulgarian party congress to the end of the party congress of the German Democratic Republic he gradually appropriated to himself the right to speak "in the name of" some seventeen parties of Latin America entirely without being authorized? The first time he did it informally in order to speak some words of greeting, the second — in Budapest — he spoke the "words of greeting," but formally and by previous arrangement. And then, in Germany, inventions and excuses as well as pressure were employed in order to arrange that the del-

egates of all the parties of Latin America would agree that
he alone would speak to the congress. One at least — the
Cuban delegate — managed to insist that he should not be
denied the right to speak. This is how the false image of
a fictitious majority in favor of a de-Leninized deformation
of the general line is being created!

You know of the condemnations of the work of the Espártaco firm, and the pressure on the party members to
stop working for the firm, but do you know of the surrepti-
tious efforts that are being made to prevent and obstruct
the distribution of the firm's products in other Latin
American countries? Here also, assiduously though silently,
the voice of militant Leninism is being silenced — and with
what right?

Chilean divisionists are at work in other countries without your knowledge. In February, at the Afro-Asian Solidarity Conference in Tanganyika, Olga Poblete was the
most active intriguer among the four revisionist divisionists
from Latin America who, improperly acting in the name
of the World Peace Council, tried to impose the will of the
revisionists on the fighters for national liberation in Asia
and Africa, slandered the authentic representatives of the
progressive fighters for the liberation of Latin America, and,
cunningly cooperating with the lackeys of the Hindu bourgeois aggressors, attempted to create conflicts and to do
spadework for the falsification and revision of the conference decisions in favor of the revisionists. . . .

Then, with superb arrogance, came an attack on the
Chilean party's policy of the Peaceful Road:

We have tried to determine the origin of these unhealthy
tendencies within the Chilean party in order to understand
ourselves and facilitate the understanding of others of what
forces create the fertile ground on which opportunism, dogmatism, and all sorts of revisionism flourish. We beg you
to make a complete examination of this fundamental question for the benefit of other communist and workers' parties,
especially in Latin America. What we ourselves have

noticed are the assiduously cultivated illusions as to the possibility of finding a painless road to power in Chile. These illusions, for which the divisionists are more and more disposed to sacrifice the basic class alliance of workers and peasants, . . . are clearly to be observed in the revisionist-reformist forces of other countries, especially in the Italian party, which are playing such a decisive part in the general attack against the sacred unity and revolutionary élan of our movement.[77]

The party declaration against Chinese propaganda literature also drew sarcastic comment from another unexpected quarter. In its issue of April 30, 1963 the Socialist afternoon tabloid *Ultima Hora* published a caustic article by its columnist Julio Silva, which said in part:

There is justified interest in getting to know the main documents that explain the Chinese point of view. These documents are now being divulged by the review *Pekin Informa*, which has recently begun to circulate in our country. In reading it certain distorted and coarse presentations of the Chinese position are dispelled, and it reveals itself, on the contrary, as very well founded on solid arguments and on a force of conviction emanating from the revolutionary fervor by which it is inspired.

But apart from the polemic itself and one's opinion of it, there is certainly no way of understanding and judging it without knowing the respective documentation. That is why it is very strange that Chilean communism has placed the Chinese publications in its "index" of forbidden or heretical books. A subtle, unobtrusive, almost ciphered communiqué warns the members against the dangerous documents, at the same time recommending, not without

[77] The complete text of the Albanian letter was published by the Conservative Santiago newspaper *Diario Ilustrado* on February 15, 1964, having been handed to the editors by members of the Spartacus group.

a certain paternalism, other safer or healthier reading matter.

. . . This zeal for stifling the debate, for avoiding the most minimal mental contamination, demonstrates the narrow and timid dogmatism of which the official communist mentality cannot rid itself. As long as it does not command state power, this strict ideological vigilance is limited to the party members, but once it has obtained this power, it is extended to the entire community. Thus . . . ideological totalitarianism is established.

In actual fact this is only a façade, since it is not so much based on a true process of persuasion as on mental compulsion through an immense machinery of pressure and deformation of the mind, of suppression of any opposition. It is strange that this dictatorship over the mind should be the heritage of two such formidable polemicists as Marx and Engels, whose thinking was formed and developed in permanent debate. . . .

This was only the beginning of a development that was to give the party leadership more cause to worry than the factional activities of the Spartacus group.

One of the owners of *Ultima Hora,* and a man who had substantial influence on its editorial policies, was Professor Clodomiro Almeyda, a member of the Chamber of Deputies and Secretary of the Santiago regional organization of the Socialist Party. At a Socialist Party seminar held earlier in April 1963 Almeyda gave a lecture on Peaceful Coexistence. Although his presentation of the Soviet interpretation of this formula was scrupulously fair, he did not hide a marked preference for the Chinese point of view.[78] Some weeks later the Socialist ideological review *Arauco*[79] published an article written

[78] A text of this lecture was published in the July 1963 issue of the Socialist ideological review *Arauco.*
[79] In its issue of May 1963.

by the Chinese theoretician Fan Ch'eng-hsiang on the intensification of the class struggle and the increasing pauperization of the working class in Western Europe. This article claimed that the contradiction between the underdeveloped countries and the imperialist bloc was "the principal contradiction" and praised Mao for "having successfully and concretely solved the peasant problem in the practice of the Chinese revolution" and for having worked out the "brilliant thesis . . . that imperialism is disintegrating more and more from day to day."

Up to this point the Chilean Communists had restricted themselves to reprinting anti-Chinese articles from the press of brother parties. Now their propagandists began to launch attacks of their own. In its issue of May–June 1963 the party ideological review *Principios* published an article by Politburo member Orlando Millas on "The Unity of the International Communist Movement." Millas declared that the Chilean Communists had always been in favor of the unity of the international movement under the leadership of the Soviet Communist Party, which was "the cradle of Leninism." Referring to the Chinese propaganda campaign, he described it as

intolerable that one should throw around scholastic arguments, pre-emptory assertions of a dogmatic nature, and fragmentary quotations from texts that refer to different circumstances, thus dislocating the gigantic mobilization of the peoples of the world against imperialist war, or sowing doubts and fomenting hesitation. . . .

Millas further declared that the Chilean party was not letting itself be provoked into an interchange of insults and attacks that would only be welcomed by the class

enemy. The party had "done everything to avoid a dis-
agreeable polemic," and it welcomed Khrushchev's
Berlin appeal to put an end to the public debate.

Only a few weeks later, Secretary-General Luis Corvalán himself made his first detailed, extensive public
attack on the Chinese. On June 6, at a plenary session
of the party's Central Committee that had ostensibly
been called to hear a report on the election campaign,
he delivered a speech on "The Differences of Opinion
with the Chinese Comrades."

Corvalán maintained that

of all the communist parties, of which there are about
ninety, only one, the Albanian Party of Labor, is totally
in accordance with the attitude of the Chinese comrades,
and two or three share it to a certain extent. . . . Therefore
these are not disagreements between the Communist Party
of China and the Communist Party of the Soviet Union.
They are disagreements between the Chinese Communist
Party, supported by the Albanians, and the entire international communist movement. . . .

After severely reproving the Chinese for their use of
abusive terms in the polemic with the Soviets Corvalán
dealt at length with the Chinese attitude toward war
and peace. He made full use of Peking's tactical mistake
of having asserted that after a new world war "the victorious peoples will very rapidly create, on the ruins of
defeated imperialism, a civilization a thousand times
superior to that existing under capitalism." He said that
this meant that "either the Chinese comrades have no
idea of what a third world war would mean, or they
harbor Olympic contempt for the life of millions and
millions of human beings. . . ." He then went on to
defend the Soviet attitude during the Caribbean crisis,

deplored the "dogmatism" and "sectarianism" of the Chinese, and made the important announcement that "Some years ago revisionism emerged as the main danger for the communist movement. But today dogmatism has become the main danger. . . ."

As for the problem of the Peaceful Road, Corvalán stressed that the evaluation of the means, conditions, and timing of the revolution in every country is "the exclusive province of the revolutionary movement of that specific country." From this he went on to discuss the state of relations between the Chinese and Chilean parties and to complain of Chinese attempts to recruit partisans among the Chilean party members:

If the Communist Party of China considers our position to be erroneous, it could address itself to the Central Committee of our party, officially presenting to us its point of view or inviting us to a bilateral conversation. This would be the proper procedure. But what has happened is that, disregarding all the norms fixed for interparty relations, it has devoted itself, as has been said, to propagating its erroneous concepts in the ranks of our party, to attempting to influence our members, to winning supporters for its line. This is without doubt an unfriendly attitude, an undermining, splitting, and disruptive activity.

The matter becomes even graver if one takes into account that in order to do this it has sought the collaboration of party members, recruited individually and against our Central Committee's will, which had been expressly made known to the Chinese comrades. The attitude of the Communist Party of China does not conform to its repeated declarations regarding the equality of all the parties.

. . . The Communist Party of Chile is one of the Latin American parties that were most active in collaborating with the Chinese comrades, especially in sending them Spanish-language teachers and literary specialists. Up to a short time ago the Chinese Communist Party used to apply to our Central Committee when in need of this type of collaboration, and its wishes were always complied with. But since about a year ago it has dispensed with this correct procedure in order to approach party members or sympathizers on its own initiative.

In view of this situation we have decided to suspend the journeys of Chilean Communists to go to work in China until the norms that have been violated by the Chinese comrades are re-established.

Referring to the Socialist *Ultima Hora*'s criticism of the party decree concerning Chinese propaganda literature, Corvalán stated that in the Chilean Communist Party

every leader or member may read whatever he wants to, including the Chinese materials. Nobody has forbidden this. But the party as such, and its individual members, may not divulge or spread political documents contrary to our own line and are in duty bound to defend, propagate, and apply the party line, which is worked out democratically. . . . Ideological liberalism has no place in our ranks since it is incompatible with political unity.

Finally, Corvalán made a humble confession of personal error:

I was in Peking early in 1959. At that time I noticed different appreciations of certain problems, as of that of the Cold War, which the Chinese comrades considered as having the virtue of stirring up the nations and contributing to their political awakening. I also noted that the Peaceful Road did not enjoy any sympathies with them. I asked for an exchange of ideas on this point with comrade Liu Shao-ch'i. I had a conversation with the responsible comrades whom I acquainted with our point of view and our concrete policy.

I thought that these different ways of looking at certain problems found their explanation in isolation, an insufficient knowledge of the international scene, a tendency to generalize their own experience. I never imagined the extent and consequences of what I was beginning to discern.

On the other hand, in not a few party documents he who is speaking to you, as well as other comrades, including comrade Galo González, have used certain Chinese formulas ("the east wind prevails over the west wind," "imperialism is a paper tiger," etc.) without fully realizing their significance. Furthermore, in my case, in a press interview given precisely on the occasion of my return from China I praised comrade Mao Tse-tung in exaggerated terms. Although comrade Víctor Galleguillos has already called attention to this in a previous plenum, I have wanted to raise it again in order to put things in their right place and to contribute to a better understanding of how complex are the problems of world revolution, and how necessary it is to delve deeper and deeper into them, to study more and more and to act more collectively.[80]

On June 14 the Chinese published their famous 25-point "Proposition Regarding the General Line of the International Communist Movement," which constituted a scathing global critique of Soviet foreign policy, of the policies of the Moscow-directed communist world movement, and of Khrushchev's ideological innovations. The Chilean Politburo reacted to this with a statement made public on July 20, 1963, in which it singled out two specific points for criticism. One of these was the Chinese statement: "If the leadership of a party adopts a nonrevolutionary line . . . its place in the revolution will be taken by the Marxist-Leninists who may exist inside or outside the party. . . ."

"This," said the Politburo's statement, "is a veritable call for the division of all those communist parties that do not share the Chinese deviation. The matter is espe-

[80] In *Principios,* September–October 1963.

cially serious because it is accompanied by actual splitting activities with the aid of factional elements expelled from the communist parties as well as with that
of mercenaries and adventurers."[81]

The Politburo statement further stressed that the
Chinese statement, "It is wrong to make peaceful coexistence the general foreign policy line of the socialist
states," was "in flagrant contradiction to the letter
and the spirit of the programmatic documents and the
principles of the international communist movement."[82]

Finally the Politburo announced that the party press
would publish both the Chinese letter of June 14 and
the Soviet reply of July 14, and that special meetings
would be held in which "the party leaders will exhaustively illuminate and denounce the erroneous views of
the Chinese comrades."[83]

Some weeks later an editorial in *Principios*[84] rather
gingerly dealt with the Chinese thesis that the underdeveloped regions of the world "constitute the storm
center of world revolution." The editorial said that this
meant "shifting the center of world revolution to the
zones of the old colonial periphery, trying to present
the role of the working class of the socialist and more
developed capitalist countries as diminished." This, the
editorial argued, would not strengthen but weaken the
peoples now struggling to liberate themselves and
would isolate the national liberation struggle. The argument was anything but convincing. Indeed, the Soviet
thesis that the "national liberation struggle" in the

[81] *El Partido Comunista de Chile y el movimiento comunista internacional, op. cit.,* p. 239.

[82] *Ibid.,* p. 240.

[83] *Ibid.,* p. 341.

[84] In its issue of September–October 1963.

"colonial and dependent countries" is secondary to the economic competition between the socialist and advanced capitalist states is to Latin American eyes by far the weakest point of the entire Soviet platform.

Up to this point the battle had been one of words. Even the one organization that the Chinese controlled in Chile, Espártaco Editores, had been concerned mainly with the distribution of printed matter. But in September 1963 the pro-Chinese elements, or, as Peking would put it, "the Marxist-Leninists inside and outside the party," moved to carry the struggle onto the organizational plane. Sometime that month posters appeared on Santiago billboards announcing two meetings to celebrate the fourteenth anniversary of the Chinese revolution. Both these meetings were to be held in Santiago cinemas on the morning of Sunday, September 29. One of them, which was to take place in the Esmeralda cinema, was organized by Vanguardia Revolucionaria Marxista, the most important group of the Chilean ultraleft (see Appendix). The other, to be held in the Baquedano cinema, was sponsored by an impressive list of FRAP personalities that included Juan Fuentealba, president of the FRAP alliance; Ana Eugenia Ugalde, a prominent member of the Chamber of Deputies and leader of the left wing of the Radicals, who had broken with her party and joined the FRAP earlier that year; Socialist Senator Alejandro Chelén; Socialist members of the Chamber of Deputies Clodomiro Almeyda and Carlos Altamirano; Julio Benítez, International Affairs Director of the Trade Union Confederation and secretary of the committee for the formation of a Latin American trade-union federation; and several other Socialist trade-union officers and journalists. Also on the

list were the names of seven Communist Party intellectuals: the Spartacus group had come out into the open.

Two days before the meetings the Communist Politburo issued a declaration stating that "certain anticommunist elements" had managed to deceive "persons of
good will" and were using their prestige in order to
stage the meetings. The declaration continued:

> The aim pursued by the promoters and organizers of
> these public functions is not to commemorate the Chinese
> revolution but to make use of the divergencies pointed out
> by the leadership of the Communist Party of Chile and the
> people's movement, to whose line they object. In other
> words, these are divisionist activities aiming to weaken the
> people's struggle and especially the candidacy of Salvador
> Allende. . . .
>
> Simultaneously with this warning, the Communist Party
> issues a call for participation in the meeting to celebrate
> the Chinese revolution, which the Sino-Chilean Cultural
> Institute has organized without any domestic political aims
> for Monday, September 30, in the ceremonial hall of the
> University of Chile.[85]

The Communist Party newspaper *El Siglo* also announced that a Communist Party delegation had visited
the headquarters of the allied Socialist Party "in order
to present the text of the declaration that its Politburo
had released to the press. . . ." It was further announced
that the Politburo had warned "the two or three" Communist Party members figuring on the list of sponsors
of the Baquedano meeting not to participate.[86]

The next day *El Siglo* was able to publish a statement
made by Senator Aniceto Rodríguez on behalf of the

---

[85] *El Siglo*, September 27, 1963.
[86] *Ibid.*

Socialist Party Central Committee announcing that this body had prohibited the participation of Socialist Party members in either of the two meetings. *El Siglo* further published statements by Juan Fuentealba and Ana Eugenia Ugalde, both of whom claimed that their names had been put on the list of sponsors (and speakers) without their knowledge.[87] A number of other prominent FRAP personalities also withdrew their names from the list.

As a further measure the Communist Party also announced an open-air mass meeting of its own to be held on the same Sunday morning in a public park only two blocks away from the Baquedano cinema. The speakers at this meeting were to be Secretary-General Luis Corvalán and Politburo member Pablo Neruda; the theme: the presidential election of 1964.

On Sunday morning, September 29, an audience of two or three hundred persons, most of them apparently students, gathered in the Baquedano cinema.[88] At the entrance stood a line of Communist Party pickets who, notebook in hand, took down the names of anyone they recognized. The flashlights of news cameras lit up the faces of the two most prominent members of the audience, Senator Alejandro Chelén and Deputy Clodomiro Almeyda, who had defied a Socialist Party order to withdraw their signatures from the list of sponsors. Also present were the former president of the Trade Union Confederation, Clotario Blest, and one of the great figures of contemporary Chilean literature, the poet Pablo de Rokha, who read a long polemical "Ode to

[87] *Ibid.*, September 28, 1963.
[88] According to press reports, attendance at the second meeting, sponsored by Vanguardia, was rather better.

China." The rostrum was decorated with huge portraits of Lenin, Mao, Fidel Castro, Ben Bella, and Lumumba.

Of the three speeches, the only one of political interest was made by Armando Cassigoli, a writer and professor of philosophy at the University of Chile, who was a Communist Party member. In what evidently was a policy statement by the Spartacus group Cassigoli criticized both the policy of Peaceful Coexistence and that of the Peaceful Road and then called for the formation of a broad "movement of support for all anti-imperialist revolutions," to be called MARA (Movimiento de Apoyo a la Revolución Anti-Imperialista).[89] MARA's principal contribution to the anti-imperialist cause was to be "to further the revolution in Chile."

Meanwhile, two blocks away in the Bustamante park, a rather meager crowd of perhaps 1,500 Communists assembled to hear their party leaders Corvalán and Neruda. As announced, Corvalán's speech dealt mainly with the election campaign. There was only one brief reference to the pro-Chinese meeting in the Baquedano theater:

> There is no danger of a split in the party. They will not be able to split one single cell, a single one of our three thousand basic organizations. Once more those who try to split our party will break their teeth as if biting on a rock. What causes us to worry is the harm which these elements may cause in the people's movement, deceiving or confusing groups or individual persons in order to create distrust among the FRAP parties and to stir up arguments among them.[90]

[89] See Armando Cassigoli, *Discurso leido por el camarada Armando Cassigoli en el acto de homenage al decimocuarto aniversario de la revolución china* (Santiago de Chile, 1963), mimeographed pamphlet.

[90] *El Siglo*, September 30, 1963.

But Pablo Neruda's speech was a violent attack on the Peking regime, the first such attack delivered by a Chilean Communist:

It seems to me that the Chinese errors and their violent internal and foreign policy stem from one sole fount: the cult of personality, internally and externally. We who have visited China have seen the case of Stalin repeated. Every street, every door, has a portrait of Mao Tse-tung. Mao Tse-tung has become a living Buddha, separated from the people by a priestly court that interprets in its own manner Marxism and the story of our times. The peasants were obliged to bow, to genuflect before the picture of the leader. Recently Comrade Chou En-lai publicly congratulated a young Chinese because he had had himself sterilized voluntarily in order to serve the cause of the Chinese Republic.

The wire from Peking said:

A Chinese peasant who had had himself sterilized in order to consecrate all his energies to the construction of socialism in China was warmly congratulated by Chou En-lai. . . . "This event has given the entire world an excellent example, especially since it is the husband who took the initiative. This example should be a great example to emulate," declared Chou En-lai.

It naturally occurs to us that if Comrade Chou En-lai's father had had this idea, Chou En-lai would not exist. Is this communism? It is rather a religious cult, ridiculous, superstitious, unacceptable.

Comrades, every railroad, every bridge, every factory, every airplane, every modern road, every agricultural cooperative in China was built by Soviet engineers and technicians. When I was there and spent some days at a resort on the Yellow Sea, two thousand Soviet technicians generously lent by the socialist state were resting in one single hotel.

And this state is accused by the Chinese leaders of not

assisting the growing forces of socialism. Those who owe everything are accusing those who gave everything.

These leaders are sending letters to every intellectual in Latin America, inciting them to collaborate in the division of the socialist world. This incitement may lead to many errors and help to weaken the national liberation fronts.

But the personality cult in China itself leads to the same tragic occurrences as in the past. Speaking only of those whom I know personally among my Chinese writer comrades, I will tell you that the foremost Chinese novelist, Lenin Prize, ex-president of the Union of Chinese Writers, Ting Ling, has disappeared. First she was condemned to wash dishes and sleep on the ground in a faraway peasants' commune. Then we did not hear of her again. I knew her very well because she was president of the committee nominated by the Ministry of Culture to receive Ilya Ehrenburg and me when we traveled to Peking in order to hand the Peace Prize to Sung Ch'ing-ling, Mrs. Sun Yat-sen. Why was she sentenced? They found out that 25 years ago she had had a love affair with a supporter of Chiang Kai-shek. Yes, this was true, but they did not say that the great writer, with her child in her arms, barefoot, and with a rifle on her shoulder, made the entire long march from Yenan to Nanking with the guerrillas of the Chinese Communist Party.

And the poet Ai Ch'ing, whom we all know in Chile, the best poet in China, an old Communist, who visited Chile on the occasion of my fiftieth birthday, where is he? Accused of being a rightist because he knows the French language, and for other ridiculous accusations, he has been banished to the Gobi desert, to an inhuman altitude, and forced to sign his poems with another name. That is, he has been morally executed.

The Chinese leader who gave me this information smiled with an icy smile.[91]

From now on, attacks on the Chinese in the Chilean

---

[91] *Ibid.*

Communist press grew so frequent that they no longer constituted events of particular significance. The ideological debate, on the other hand, was not resumed until December, when *Problems of Peace and Socialism* published a new article on the Peaceful Road by Luis Corvalán, his third on the subject. This dealt in part with a letter that the Chinese Communist Party had sent to the Chilean Central Committee. Corvalán quoted the following sentence from the Chinese letter:

> In Latin America the Peaceful Road that you advocate stands in marked contrast to the Revolutionary Road of Fidel Castro and other comrades, who have led the Cuban people to victory.

To this, Corvalán replied

> We cannot but underline that the problem of the strategic and tactical line to be followed, including the matter of the road, as well as the moment when the masses shall be launched into the decisive battle, is the concern of each particular communist party of the revolutionaries of each particular country. The revolutionaries of one or the other country run the risk of committing mistakes in the elaboration or application of their line, but since they operate on terrain that they know, they have fewer possibilities of erring than revolutionaries from outside who might present themselves as gratuitous advisers. And on the other hand, the masses and their vanguard in every country can work their line out correctly only in the light of the laws of the revolutionary process, mainly by their own experience.
> The leaders of the Communist Party of China have dedicated themselves to the dishonest game of presenting matters as if they were partisans of the armed road and the other parties partisans of the peaceful road. As part of this game they try to contrast our revolutionary process with the Cuban revolutionary process. All this is absurd. No

communist party that accepts the thesis of the peaceful road rejects a priori the armed road. Even more, there are parties that in their own country follow the armed road and are at the same time against the positions of the Communist Party of China, which denies the theoretical-practical value of the peaceful road thesis. This, for example, is the case of the Communist Party of Paraguay and of various Central American parties.

The significance of the Cuban revolution as an example of heroism and as a palpable demonstration that all the peoples of the continent can liberate themselves if they struggle with determination and rely on international solidarity, in the first place of the socialist world, is very great. Constant support for this revolution *coincides with the cause* of the peoples of the entire continent. And those who try to speculate about objective tactical differences in order to promote differences of another kind do not assist, but work against, this cause.

Generally speaking, the content of the revolution in every Latin American country is the same. All the peoples of Latin America will follow the Cuban example in liberating themselves from imperialism, in liquidating the big estates and the other barriers to the development of the productive forces, in making the cultural revolution, and in taking the road to socialism. But as to the forms and means of reaching these goals, there are and will necessarily be differences. All Marxist-Leninists are agreed that every revolutionary process has its own particularities.

The tendency to copy this or that revolutionary process mechanically is at best subjectivism. Both in theory and in daily practice the revolutionaries must not be guided only by their good intentions but by the concrete circumstances within which they operate. If there are no circumstances that makes for mass support of the revolution, then there can be no revolution. . . .[92]

Corvalán failed to mention that besides "tactical differences of an objective nature" there was a very

[92] Translated from *Nuestra Epoca*, December 1963.

serious difference of opinion on international policy between the Cubans and all those communist parties that, like the Chilean party, support the Soviet line.

When Fidel Castro returned from his trip to the Soviet Union, where he had spent the entire month of May 1963, the Chilean party newspaper *El Siglo* printed, in thirteen installments, the full text of the enthusiastic marathon speech he had made on Havana television. The general impression of this speech, and of the joint communiqué issued after Castro's talks with Khrushchev, was highly favorable to the Soviet Union in spite of the fact that Castro had carefully avoided any attack on China or Albania and had even explicitly defended the Chinese against the charge of warmongering. He had said

The imperialists have lied on every point. As regards peaceful coexistence [they say] that we have supported the Soviet thesis against the Chinese. Who says that the Chinese thesis is the war thesis? . . . There is no one, there is no communist who wants war.[93]

But this little detail went unnoticed in the flood of praise that Castro bestowed on the Soviet Union and on Khrushchev personally. *El Siglo* itself in an editorial on July 17, 1963 declared

Fidel Castro's trip to Moscow liquidated the last vestiges of misunderstanding between Cuba and the Soviet Union (and it is significant that the Chinese press has devoted such scant attention to this trip). . . . Fidel himself had to admit in memorable speeches that Soviet support had been as decisive for the salvation of Cuba as the decision and heroism of the Cuban people. . . .

This same editorial also dealt with the test ban

[93] *El Siglo*, June 19, 1963.

negotiations that had just begun in Moscow — "negotiations of the greatest importance." But when the governments of the socialist camp later lined up to sign the test ban treaty, not only China but also Cuba were not among them. The Chilean Communist press hid this from its readers and did not print or comment on the speech in which Cuba's U.N. delegate stated his government's negative attitude toward the treaty.

The joint communiqué issued in January 1964, after Castro's second trip to the Soviet Union, was given very poor play in *El Siglo*. The reason for this was undoubtedly that the communiqué did not contain what the Chilean Communist leaders were looking for — a condemnation of China or even Albania, or at least an announcement that Cuba was now willing to sign the test ban treaty. Now the test ban issue was really the issue of Peaceful Coexistence, and Castro's silence meant that on this issue also, as on the issue of the Peaceful Road, he was really on the Chinese side even if he did not openly say so.

However, 1964 was an election year in Chile, and as the election campaign reached its height the Cuban and Chinese issues temporarily faded into the background, and even the most determined opponents of the Peaceful Road policy joined in the effort to install a revolutionary regime by peaceful means. In the Socialist Party the pro-Chinese leftists' attempt to take over the leadership was easily foiled by Raúl Ampuero. Nor did the Spartacus group prosper. After the meeting in the Baquedano cinema its ringleaders had been publicly expelled, and a quiet purge had eliminated their known supporters from the Communist Party and the Communist Youth. They had not been able to form the broad Movement of Support for the Anti-Imperial-ist Revolution that they had planned. In spite of Chinese financial backing Spartacus now appeared to deteriorate into just one more of the minute, quarrel-some, and completely unimportant sects that pullulate in the far-out territory beyond the fringes of the Com-munist and Socialist parties — the "soda-fountain guerrillas," as Socialist leader Raúl Ampuero sarcasti-cally called them.

Democratic sentiment is so strong in Chile that even the wildest of these fringe groups did not dare to go against it by continuing to insist on the impossibility of achieving socialism by the Peaceful Road. As the date of the election grew nearer, all of them consider-ably toned down their criticism of the "reformist" Socialist and Communist Party leaderships and actively participated in Allende's campaign.

For the Communist Party leadership, this was but a brief respite. It was easy to foresee that the truce be-tween the pro-Chinese and the pro-Soviet elements of the Chilean Left would not survive an election defeat.

4

NATIONALISM AND SOCIALISM IN THE POLICIES OF THE SOCIALIST PARTY OF CHILE

RELATIONS WITH THE COMMUNISTS

At first glance the relations between the Socialists and the Communists in Chile appear to be strikingly similar to those prevailing in Italy in the late 1940's and early 1950's, with the Socialist presidential candidate Salvador Allende playing much the same subservient role vis-à-vis Communist Secretary-General Luis Corvalán as Pietro Nenni once played vis-à-vis Palmiro Togliatti. The temptation to compare the Chilean and Italian Socialists has become even greater since both parties have developed a pro-Chinese wing. Yet in spite of this development the resemblance is superficial. The Chilean Socialists are in a far stronger, less dependent position than their Italian comrades were at the time of their bondage to the Communists.

In Chile there is no mass infiltration of the Socialist Party by the Communists. Many Communists joined the Socialists when their own party was banned, but the vast majority of them pulled out again when the Communists regained their legality. Even in Chile, where the Communists are stronger than anywhere else in South America, the scarcity of cadres is one of their greatest problems; and so, in order to rebuild their own party organization, they had to withdraw from that of the Socialists. The restoration of the Communist Party's legality thus had the salutary effect of flushing the Communists out of other organizations that they had infiltrated. The Chilean Socialists are not financially dependent on subsidies from Communist-dominated cooperatives and trade unions, as they once were in Italy. In Chile the cooperative movement is rudimentary, and the trade unions are financially so weak that in most unions the political parties have to pay the salaries of the staff, and not vice versa.[1]

The numerical relations between the two parties are also much less favorable to the Communists in Chile than in Italy. Whereas in Italy the voting strength of the Socialists was and still is not much more than half that of the Communists, in Chile it is nearly equal — 11.1 per cent to the Communists' 12.4 per cent in the municipal elections of 1963. This inevitably gives the Socialists better standing within the various bodies in which they cooperate with the Communists — FRAP committees, municipal administrations, trade unions, and so on — than they ever enjoyed in Italy.

Furthermore personal relations between Socialists and Communists on every level from the central

[1] See the chapter on the labor movement in Robert J. Alexander's *Today's Latin America* (New York: Doubleday, 1962). Most of the remarks he makes about Latin American trade unions in general apply to Chile in particular.

leadership down to the municipalities are far less cordial in Chile than they were, and often still are, in Italy. Chile was spared the horrors of fascism, world war, and German occupation. In consequence the political differences between Socialists and Communists are not alleviated by the bond of a common antifascist resistance mystique. On the contrary, the entire history of the relations between the two parties is one of bitter rivalry, which has been only muted, but by no means eliminated, during periods of political collaboration. There is no love lost between the top-ranking party leaders, and fierce competition and animosity prevail in the union locals and municipalities.

In spite of this situation majority opinion in the Socialist Party appears to be in favor of maintaining the alliance with the Communists. The Socialist Party leaders consistently disregard warnings by European and North American socialist friends, who point out that in other parts of the world the communists' superior organization and discipline have almost invariably enabled them to reduce their allies to the state of helpless satellites. But perhaps these warnings do not sufficiently take into account the specific conditions prevailing in Latin America. The Chilean Socialist leaders are not starry-eyed political novices. They certainly harbor no illusions as to the Communists' aims and intentions in maintaining the alliance. Every single one of them has a long record of political struggle against the Communists. It is true that organizationally the Chilean Communists are greatly superior to the Socialists; but in intensely individualistic Latin America, organizational superiority somehow does not weigh quite so heavily as in other parts of the world. Latin American organizations may look impressive on paper, but they are not very effective in practice since there is not enough discipline, devotion, and self-sacrifice behind them; hence the scarcity of cadres, of real activists, with which even such a large communist party as that of Chile is afflicted.

Yet even granted that the Chilean Socialists have some reason to be confident of their ability to hold their own within the FRAP alliance, there still remains the question why they should deem this alliance to be necessary, and why they prefer it to collaboration with nonsocialist, democratic parties of the Left and Center. In order to understand this, it is necessary to examine the Socialist Party's historical and ideological background.

SOME ASPECTS OF SOCIALIST PARTY HISTORY

As we have noted, Chilean political terminology is borrowed from Europe, but the institutions and situations to which it is applied are very different from those encountered in the Old World, a fact that creates the most dangerous of all the pitfalls awaiting the European or North American student of Chilean affairs. He is given an entirely erroneous feeling of familiarity and thus tricked into evaluating the political scene by mere analogy instead of serious analysis.

Thus the fact that besides the Communists there is in Chile a second working-class party that calls itself Socialist and proclaims its ideology to be Marxism naturally leads the foreign observer to assume that this is a social democratic party of the familiar European type. The Chilean Socialists were for a long time victims to a similar but opposite illusion in believing that the European socialists had some affinity with them. However, both sides finally found out that they had nothing in common, and the Chilean Socialists' relations with the Socialist International were broken off.

One of the decisive differences is that the Chilean Socialist Party does not reach back into the years before the First World War and thus lacks the European socialists' long tradition of activity as the democratic party of the working class. The original Chilean Socialist Workers' Party, founded in 1912, joined the Comintern and changed its name to Communist Party in 1921. For a full ten years the Communists more or less monopolized the political movement of the Marxist Left.

It was only after the downfall of General Ibáñez' dictatorial government in 1931 that independent socialist groups emerged.[2] The five groups that later merged to form the Socialist Party undoubtedly appeared on the scene because the Communist Party was at that time passing through the worst phase of third period ultraleftism and thus was completely incapable of giving any kind of guidance to the Chilean Left. Although the founders of these groups were not ex-Communists, Chilean Socialism may be said to be the product of dissatisfaction with Communist leadership of the Left, whereas in most European countries communism was a secession from the older, socialist stem.

The Chilean Communists have not a single revolutionary rising on their record. The birth act of the Chilean Socialist Party, on the other hand, was a real revolution: the military rising of June 4, 1932, which led to the establishment of a short-lived Socialist

[2] See Senator Alejandro Chelén Rojas' article, "El Partido Socialista de Chile," in *Arauco* No. 40, May 1963.

Republic. The rising was staged by that amiable romantic, Colonel Marmaduke Grove, chief of the Chilean air force, who had as his civilian adviser Eugenio Matte Hurtado, a Socialist intellectual who was also Grand Master of the Chilean Masons. Marmaduke Grove and his fellow officers were Latin American nationalists of a stamp of mind not unlike that of the army group that twelve years later seized power in Argentina under the leadership of Colonel Juan Perón and established the reign of Justicialism. Grove lacked the drive, political instinct, and skill to play a similar role, but he was undoubtedly a precursor of Justicialism.[3] Nationalism and Justicialism thus stood at the cradle of the Chilean Socialist Party, and they have accompanied it ever since. This is certainly the reason why the party has always found sympathizers in the officers' corps, which is strongly nationalistic and middle class and therefore antioligarchic. Yet the Communist Party appears to count few if any adherents in the Chilean army.

An ambitious rival deposed Grove and Matte after only twelve days and shipped them off to faraway Easter Island, Chile's possession in the Pacific. Later that year democracy was restored, and Grove returned to run for president. He lost the election to Arturo Alessandri, the candidate of the Center and moderate Left, but his vote was surprisingly high, and this encouraged the five socialist groups that had backed him to amalgamate into the Socialist Party of Chile, which was officially founded early in 1933.

During the twelve days of his Socialist Republic

[3] Eudocio Ravines, in his *América Latina: un continente en erupción* (Buenos Aires: Editorial Claridad, S. A., 1956), lists Grove as a "frustrated Justicialist."

the Communists had treated Grove as a Chilean Kerensky. Later, during his presidential campaign, they denounced him as "objectively defending imperialism and feudalism by not proposing expropriation without indemnification of all foreign-owned enterprises" and claimed that his movement was becoming "increasingly fascist."[4] But these accusations were ineffectual. Within a year or two of its founding the Socialist Party had obtained control of the majority of the trade unions and had become the principal party of the Chilean working class, whereas the Communists for the time being remained a small and powerless sect.

The Popular Front policy of the late 1930's enabled the Communists to recover and almost proved the Socialists' undoing. As we have seen, the Chilean Popular Front was not an alliance to stop fascism but merely an electoral coalition for the purpose of bringing the mildly left-of-center Radical Party to power and giving it control over government patronage, if need be even with the help of fascist votes. By their association with the Radicals the Communists regained the respectability they had gambled away by the wild extravagance of their third period ultraleftism, but their real reasons for promoting the Popular Front were undoubtedly that they had been ordered to do so by the Comintern and that the success of the Popular Front greatly increased their standing with that body.

These reasons were not valid for the Socialists. They had never lost their political respectability, and as a purely Chilean party they did not take orders from abroad and did not have to worry about their standing

[4] Robert J. Alexander, *Communism in Latin America* (2nd printing; New Brunswick, N.J.: Rutgers University Press, 1960), p. 180.

in Moscow. They were therefore not really interested in the alliance with the Radicals and did not see why they should help that party to win the presidency. They thus insisted that their own leader, Marmaduke Grove, be the presidential candidate of the Popular Front even if this meant a break with the Radicals. But in the crucial session of the Popular Front convention the Communists voted for the Radicals' nominee, Pedro Aguirre Cerda. The Socialists bitterly resented this.

In his autobiography the veteran Communist Elías Lafertte attributes Socialist resistance against Aguirre Cerda's candidacy to the influence of the Trotskyist group of Manuel Hidalgo, which had recently joined the Socialist Party,[5] but in reality the entire Socialist leadership was uniformly opposed to the nomination of Aguirre Cerda. According to Lafertte the Socialists' anger at the Communists was so great that when he rose to speak at a Popular Front meeting his voice was drowned out by Socialist catcalls. Lafertte further relates that one of the Radical leaders, Gabriel González Videla, then jumped up in his defense, took off his jacket, and only with difficulty was prevented from coming to blows with the Socialist leader Marmaduke Grove.[6] This was the same Gabriel González Videla who years later had the Communist Party outlawed.

At first glance the Chilean Socialists' reluctance to accept the Radicals as leaders of the Popular Front would appear to have been due to the same doctrinaire spirit that before and even after the First World War prevented many European socialist parties from collab-

---

[5] Elías Lafertte, *Vida de un comunista* (*paginas autobiográficas*) (Santiago de Chile: Talleres Gráficos Horizonte, 1961), p. 304.
[6] *Ibid.*, pp. 306 f.

orating with non-Marxist parties. But in reality the Chilean Socialists' attitude was dictated by considerations of a purely practical nature. The Radicals were their competitors for influence among white-collar workers, school teachers, and even in the labor movement, where they still controlled a number of unions. The Radicals were a very strong and immensely power-and-patronage-hungry party; it was most unlikely that after victory they would afford the Socialists a fair share of the spoils. As we have seen, the antifascist bond uniting the Popular Front was a mere myth. The parties of the Popular Front were not driven together by a common enemy who threatened them with annihilation. Furthermore the Radicals had little desire to implement a program of sweeping social reforms.

In terms of Chilean politics the alliance with the Radicals did not really make sense for the Socialists. They allowed themselves to be dragged into it under the hypnotic effect of European political slogans that had no relevance to the Chilean political situation, and thus from the beginning they felt cheated and dissatisfied. This is how one of their ideologists, Oscar Waiss, later summed up the Popular Front:

The Popular Front was a gigantic political error that saved the Radical Party from falling apart, deprived the masses of their revolutionary initiative, and held up the offensive of the workers for a long period. The Popular Front was an act of social legerdemain that transformed the people's aspirations into mere verbalism and never was intended to modify the structure of landed property or to retrieve the ownership of our natural resources. Instead it increased the already excessive proliferation of bureaucracy by incorporating thousands of petty-bourgeois elements into the state administration and wasting the energies of the nation in a multitude of new, ineffective, and inoperative organisms. One after the other, and with uniformly increasing speed, the Radical governments led to new disappointments and to mounting resentment of the masses against the parties and men responsible for cheating the people out of fulfillment of their true and deep desires.[7]

The events after Aguirre Cerda's victory fully justified the Socialists' qualms. They had to be satisfied with three minor cabinet posts and with the same privilege that the Radicals had enjoyed under the preceding Alessandri administration, namely, to quote Eudocio Ravines' picturesque phrase, that of "wiping their mouths while their Radical ally ate and drank."[8] Very soon opposition against further participation made itself felt within the party. In the eight-year period covered by the administrations of the two Radical Presidents, Aguirre Cerda and Juan Antonio Ríos, several open splits occurred in the party. In 1946 the Socialists finally decided to sever connections with the Radicals and to contest the presidential election of that year with a candidate of their own, while the Communist-Radical alliance continued with the Communists backing the Radical candidate Gabriel González Videla. But by that time the Socialists had already been greatly weakened by constant internal dissension. González Videla won the election, with the Socialist candidate coming in a bad fourth.

Besides their three cabinet seats in the new government the Communists also obtained President González Videla's backing in their efforts to wrest control of the labor movement from the Socialists. For the next year

[7] Oscar Waiss, *Nacionalismo y socialismo en América Latina* (2nd ed.; Buenos Aires: Ediciones Iguazú, 1961), pp. 138 f.
[8] See Chapter 3, p. 48.

or so there was literally a state of war between the Socialists and the Communists, with frequent street battles between the strong-arm squads that both sides employed.[9]

After González Videla had turned against his Communist allies and ejected them from the cabinet he invited the Socialists to join his government. But the old-guard party leaders who accepted this invitation no longer enjoyed control over the party. As early as 1946 they had lost control to a group of younger party leaders headed by Raúl Ampuero, the president of the Socialist Youth.[10] This led to another schism in 1948, with the bulk of the party following Ampuero to form the Partido Socialista Popular, while the old guard with a small band of followers retained the name Partido Socialista de Chile.

According to Raúl Ampuero[11] the issue between the two groups was that the old-guard leaders were so embittered by the struggle with the Communists as to be willing to accept the Right as an ally against them, whereas he and his group argued that the Communists could be defeated only "from the Left," that is, by taking an even more radical course than they. This position of course precluded participation in the González Videla government. But this negative attitude of the Partido Socialista Popular was dictated by reasons of expedience, not of principle. The party was not against collaboration with non-Marxist groups and participation in "bourgeois" governments per se. This was clearly demonstrated in 1952, when the Partido So-

[9] Alexander, *Communism in Latin America, op. cit.,* pp. 199 ff.
[10] *Ibid.,* p. 204; also Alejandro Chelén, in *Arauco,* No. 40, May 1963.
[11] In a statement to the author on January 3, 1964 in Santiago.

cialista Popular backed the candidacy of ex-dictator Ibáñez in the presidential election and then joined the victor's government.

General Carlos Ibáñez del Campo had an unsavory record as dictator in the years 1926–1931, when numerous Communists and representatives of the democratic parties were relegated to remote islands or banished from the country. Later he had been associated with González von Marées' Nazi Party and other fascist groups. His speeches in the 1952 presidential election campaign inveighed against parliament and the political parties and had definite fascist overtones. Ibáñez was a personal friend of the Argentinian dictator Juan Perón, and both his supporters and his opponents expected his victory in the 1952 election to result in the installation of an antiparliamentarian, Peronista type of regime.

The foreign observer will find it well-nigh impossible to comprehend how the majority group of the Chilean Socialists could support such a man and even join his government. When Robert J. Alexander asked Socialist Secretary-General Raúl Ampuero for an explanation, he was given to understand that the Socialist leaders "felt that Ibáñez was going to win anyway, and that the Partido Socialista Popular could influence the movement by joining it, but would be crushed if it attempted to buck the Ibañista forces."[12]

However, this highly opportunistic argument does not suffice to explain how a leftist party that found it difficult to collaborate with the left-of-center democratic Radicals could bring itself to join a movement of fascist or at least authoritarian and antiparliamentarian tendency. To solve this puzzle one must completely dis-

[12] Alexander, *Communism in Latin America, op. cit.*, p. 206.

card the European concept of fascism as a movement of the extreme Right. The Latin American "fascism" of such figures as Perón, Ibáñez, or the Getulio Vargas of the 1930's does not occupy the same position in the political spectrum as fascism of the familiar European type.

In Europe fascism developed as a movement to "save the country from bolshevism." In consequence it enjoyed the sympathies and support of many financiers, industrialists, and big landowners. To European eyes this connection with the oligarchy places fascism on the extreme right of the political spectrum.

Latin American "fascism," however, although it employs the terminology and most of the techniques of its European namesake, is not primarily anticommunist but antioligarchic. The oligarchy of such European countries as Germany, France, and Italy is traditionally somewhat less than enthusiastic about parliamentary democracy and thus approved of fascism's campaign against parliamentary corruption. The Latin American oligarchy of such countries as Argentina, Brazil, and Chile traditionally uses parliamentary democracy as its instrument of rule. The antiparliamentarian demagoguery of such "fascist" or authoritarian politicians as Vargas, Perón, or Ibáñez, though superficially similar to the phraseology of European fascism, was therefore aimed at a very different target: Its purpose was to wrest control of the government from the oligarchy.

There is yet another very important difference between European fascism and Latin American "fascism," or, to use a more appropriate term, Justicialism. The former was nihilistic in its Nietzschean proclamation of the right of the strong to subjugate the weak. Justicialism, on the other hand, came out for the equality and dignity of the common man. As Robert J. Alexander writes in his *Prophets of the Revolution:*

. . . Perón came to power in the face of the opposition of the principal elements of the *status quo ante* instead of with their help, as in the cases of Italy and Germany. The large landholders, the industrialists, and most other elements of the Argentine upper classes were violently opposed to Perón, and most of them remained so throughout his tenure in office. . . . He fundamentally changed the balance of power in Argentina, ending forever the control over the nation by the rural landlords who had dominated it for more than a century. He gave a status to the urban and rural working class which no successor regime could take away from them, even if it wanted to. The organized-labor movement became a permanent element of key importance in the power structure of Argentina, and the workingmen had a feeling of having "arrived," which never could be entirely taken away from them.[13]

The Latin American noncommunist but Marxist Left and the "fascist" or Justicialist movements of the Peronista type thus have much in common — including a ferocious nationalism. What keeps them apart is really only that each uses a different, antagonistic terminology that is imported from Europe and has no real bearing on the Latin American scene.

But terminology is no insurmountable barrier to cooperation. That is why the Chilean Socialists were far less reluctant to collaborate with the authoritarian, semifascist Ibáñez than with the democratic Radical Party. In addition there was probably also another, more prosaic reason: Since there was a scarcity of

[13] Robert J. Alexander, *Prophets of the Revolution: Profiles of Latin American Leaders* (New York: Macmillan, 1962), pp. 265 f.

political talent and experience in the large amorphous Ibáñez movement, the Socialists could hope to play a far more important part in this movement, and later in the Ibáñez government, than they had under Radical leadership in the Popular Front.

Ibáñez' sweeping victory in the 1952 presidential election was hailed by the Socialists as a "peaceful revolution,"[14] but their hopes failed to materialize. As a rabble rouser Ibáñez could not compare with Perón. He was unable to, and probably did not want to, build up a personal following among the dispossessed. He did not carry out the sweeping program of nationalization of industry and the agrarian reform envisaged by the Socialists, which would have alienated his more conservative supporters and forced him to depend on the Left. He preferred a skillful game of playing various groups and personalities off against each other. Hence the frequent changes in his cabinet, which underwent total reconstruction no less than twelve times in the course of his six-year presidential term, with 135 different personalities serving in his ministries.[15]

At one stage Ibáñez encouraged a military group to plan a coup that would have rid him of parliamentary supervision. The conspirators, the so-called "Linea Recta" group, were officers with Socialist sympathies, and a number of Socialist Party leaders were in the know.[16] The coup failed to materialize because the

[14] Ernesto Würth Rojas, *Ibáñez, caudillo enigmático* (Santiago de Chile: Editorial Del Pacífico, S. A., 1958), p. 279.
[15] *Ibid.*, pp. 335 ff.
[16] Statement by Oscar Waiss to author in an interview on February 7, 1964.

top army leaders took a firm stand against it, and possibly also because Ibáñez was not too keen to let it succeed but only wanted to use it to frighten the parliamentary opposition into subservience. So the highly authoritarian Ibáñez finally came to the end of his term of office without having violated the constitution — a remarkable demonstration of the strength of democratic institutions and democratic traditions in Chile.

The Socialists had withdrawn from the government before the first year of the administration was out and then gradually passed from a position of qualified support to one of open opposition. But their opposition was not quite so determined as that of the Radical Party. In 1957, when the Chamber of Deputies had to vote on a Radical motion to impeach the president for having jeopardized the honor and security of the country by his close relations with the Argentinian government of Juan Perón, the Socialist deputies abstained.[17]

With their estrangement from the Ibañista movement, the Socialists had to look for new allies. In 1957 they reunited with the old-guard splinter group, which in a surprising turn had meanwhile switched from violent anticommunism to collaboration with the Communists,[18] who had supported its candidate Dr. Salvador Allende in the 1952 presidential election.[19] The reunited party, which was dominated by Raúl Ampuero, recovered its traditional name of Socialist Party of

---

[17] Würth Rojas, *op. cit.*, p. 351.

[18] See Chapter 3, p. 58.

[19] Allende had come in a bad fourth, polling 50,000 votes against Ibáñez' 446,000.

Chile. Next year it joined up with the Communists and some Ibañista splinter groups to form the Popular Action Front (FRAP).

FRAP was a very different alliance from the old Popular Front, which was dominated by the non-Marxist Radicals, with the Communists acting as campaign managers and the Socialists being dragged along as a reluctant third partner. The Popular Front had been a broad alliance with a strong non-Marxist element and a diluted program, which was very much to the Communists' liking. The Socialists, on the other hand, were most unhappy in the Popular Front. They resented the overpowering presence of the non-Marxist Radicals and would have much preferred a narrower, proletarian, and hence more aggressive formation. FRAP was exactly this narrower, proletarian formation, with only an insignificant non-Marxist element, that the Socialists had dreamed of in 1938. And this time it was the Communists who were uneasy, since they would have liked a broader, more diluted alliance.

In the opinion of the Socialist Party the presidential election of 1958 proved the viability of the FRAP formula of a narrow, proletarian alliance. In this election the victorious candidate of the Liberals and Conservatives, Jorge Alessandri, polled only 40,000 votes more than the FRAP candidate Allende, who came in well ahead of the Christian Democrat and Radical candidates. Allende's sensationally high vote silenced those Socialists who, for reasons of principle or expediency, had opposed collaboration with the Communists. They no longer had an effective voice in the determination of party policy. Although there was still no love lost between the Socialists and the Communists, collaboration with the Communists was no longer an issue in the Socialist Party. Division inside the party from now on ran along different lines.

POLITICAL FASHION AND
THE CHILEAN SOCIALISTS

Looking at the history of the Chilean Socialist Party, one is struck by a feature in which it differs both from its Communist ally and competitor and from the socialist parties of the Old World: its extreme susceptibility to political fashions imported either from other continents or from other Latin American countries.

The Socialist Party started out in 1933 with a strong anticommunist bias. In its first years it nearly succeeded in depriving the sectarian Communists of what little influence they still had among the Chilean working class. But when the Communists changed their line and stretched out the hand of friendship, it very soon gave in to their wooing and even joined the Popular Front coalition with the non-Marxist Radicals. As we have already seen, the Socialists' alliance with the Radicals did not make sense from a Chilean point of view, and indeed they gained nothing from it and were greatly weakened by their participation. They had seen this clearly from the beginning, and if they allowed themselves to be dragged into the alliance against their better judgment, this can be explained only by the fact that the Popular Front, after its successes in France and Spain, was *the* great fashion with leftists all over the world. To refuse to join it would have made the Chilean Socialists appear parochial in other Chileans' eyes and in their own.

In 1946 the Socialists finally made up their mind to break with the Popular Front. Meanwhile a new star had arisen on the Latin American political horizon. In 1945 Colonel Juan Perón had assumed power in neighboring Argentina. The Chilean Socialists were quickly drawn into his orbit. They admired him for his struggle against the democratic political parties, which were regarded by them as instruments of the oligarchy, and also, with some justification, for his labor legislation and encouragement of the labor movement.

When Perón was overthrown in 1955, the details of high living and corruption that were made public by his victorious opponents completely discredited him outside his own country. Overnight, Peronism went out of fashion in Latin America. But the Chilean Socialists immediately found a new fashion to follow.

Khrushchev's trip to Belgrade in May 1955 and his sensational confession of Soviet errors aroused the Chilean Socialists' interest in Titoism. As early as July of that year the Foreign Relations Secretary of the Socialist Party, Oscar Waiss, and Socialist Senator Aniceto Rodríguez arrived in Belgrade. They had meetings with Tito, Kardelj, Ranković, Vukmanović, and other Yugoslav leaders and were initiated into the workings of the communes and the workers' councils. After his return, Oscar Waiss summed up his impressions:

I had learned a great lesson. A lesson of quiet heroism, of efficiency and of modesty, of titanic effort and thrift. . . . I had learned a lesson, the import of which I could not yet fully appreciate but which would bear fruit in time in my own activity as a fighter for socialism.[20]

[20] In Oscar Waiss, *Amanecer en Belgrado* (Santiago de Chile: Prensa Latinoamericana, S. A., 1956), p. 158.

After the Soviet Communist Party's renewed break with Yugoslavia in April 1958 the Chilean Socialists' fascination with Titoism inevitably caused stresses and strains in their new alliance with the Communists. As early as July of that year Communist Secretary-General Luis Corvalán noted with displeasure:

It is also very much in evidence that in the Socialist Party there are influential people who do not hide their sympathies for Yugoslav revisionism. . . . In every case where topical theoretical and political problems, and specifically Yugoslav revisionism, definitively have a practical significance, it becomes necessary to point to the danger involved in differences of opinion about these matters, and to the need for the most determined efforts to overcome them.[21]

Later that year the Eleventh National Congress of the Communist Party adopted a resolution that said in part: "The congress considers that revisionism is at present the most dangerous manifestation of the influence exerted by the exploiting classes within the Chilean workers' and people's movement."[22] In his main speech at that congress Luis Corvalán deplored that "Yugoslav revisionism has some disciples . . . inside the Chilean workers' and people's movement." He warned that "if these revisionist opinions were to spread further in the Chilean workers' and people's movement, this would lead to . . . conciliation and to a kind of 'third position' that has at times served as cover for the most rabid anticommunism."[23] In a public speech summing up the proceedings of the party congress, Politburo member Orlando Millas once more gave

[21] *Principios*, July–August 1958.
[22] Partido Comunista de Chile, *Documentos del XI Congreso Nacional realizado en noviembre de 1958* (Santiago de Chile: Talleres Gráficos Lautaro, 1959), p. 140.
[23] *Ibid.*, pp. 73 f.

vent to the party's indignation at the pro-Yugoslav attitude of the Socialist leaders:

. . . conformity with this revisionism and rancorous anti-Sovietism cannot be explained merely as a consequence of some people having read Yugoslav texts, but only as a concrete manifestation of the influence of imperialism or at least of bourgeois elements on certain politicians of the people's camp.[24]

The following year the Communist Party publishing house even brought out a book designed to combat the nefarious influence of Titoism on the Chilean workers' and people's movement. This was *El problema yugoslavo,* a 285-page collection of Chilean Communist Party statements and anti-Yugoslav diatribes by foreign communist ideologists.

Characteristically the Chilean Socialists were not impressed by these harangues and attempts at intimidation. They proudly proclaimed their adherence to the Titoist foreign policy principle of the "third position" outside the two camps, and at one point they even ordered the Chilean Socialist delegates to resign from the Communist-sponsored World Peace Council, thereby provoking Luis Corvalán to a veritable paroxysm of rage.[25] Finally, Communist pressure subsided without any ideological concessions on the Socialist side. Today the book *El problema yugoslavo* is a source of embarrassment to the Communists, especially because it includes two violent Chinese pronouncements against "contemporary revisionism."

Relations between the Chilean Socialists and the

24 *Ibid.,* p. 74.
25 See Luis Corvalán's speeches of May 10, 1959 and May 17, 1959 in his *Chile y el nuevo panorama mundial* ([Santiago de Chile]: Talleres Gráficos Lautaro, 1959).

League of Communists of Yugoslavia are friendly to this day. Articles by Yugoslav ideologists appear in the Chilean Socialist review *Arauco*; the Socialist Party publishing house, Prensa Lationoamericana, has published and continues to distribute translations of the Yugoslav party program and of Edvard Kardelj's "Socialist Democracy in Yugoslav Practice";[26] Yugoslav guest delegates attend Chilean Socialist Party celebrations and congresses, and the Secretary-General of the Socialist Party, Raúl Ampuero, is still a fervent Titoist. Yet in spite of all this, Titoism can no longer be said to be the dominant ideological influence in the Socialist Party of Chile. Since 1960 it has steadily lost ground to a new influence of far greater appeal to the Latin American mind.

Socialist Senator Salvador Allende in July 1960 in a Senate speech devoted to Cuba said

The Chilean people have been aroused and deeply moved by the Cuban revolution: they understand it and defend it as their own. . . . The parties of the people, and, with some reticence, even center parties, have declared their support of the revolution. This means that the immense majority of the Chileans is for the revolution. It is time to realize that the lesson of Guatemala has been learnt. The United States must understand that today Latin America is revitalized by the Cuban revolution. With different methods and strategies, in accordance with the characteristics of each one of our countries, we are marching toward a common goal that shall give dignity to our lives and assure the economic independence of our countries.[27]

As the Cuban regime became more extremist and

[26] Edvard Kardelj, *La democracia socialista en la práctica yugoslava* (Santiago de Chile: Prensa Latinoamericana, S. A.).

[27] Salvador Allende, *Cuba, un camino* (Santiago de Chile: Prensa Latinoamericana, 1960), p. 55.

drew ever closer to communism, the Latin American
moderates who had enthusiastically supported it in
1959 and 1960 gradually turned away in disappoint-
ment. But the effect on the Chilean Socialists was quite
the opposite: Their own policy grew more radical in
keeping with that of the Cubans. A similar development took place in the Communist Party, and this led
to a rapid radicalization of the FRAP alliance as a
whole. The clamor of FRAP propagandists for the
immediate expropriation of foreign holdings and for
a drastic agrarian reform grew ever stronger. The FRAP
leaders still insisted that in the event of a FRAP victory
in the election of 1964 they would install a "people's
regime" and not a full-scale socialist one. Yet the
political and economic reforms envisaged in the FRAP
electoral program for 1964 were so sweeping that they
could certainly not be implemented within the framework of Chile's existing democratic institutions. That
program envisaged, *inter alia,* nationalization of foreign-
owned copper, nitrate, and iron ore resources; an
agrarian reform destined to ensure that "the land belongs to those who work it"; nationalization of all banks
and insurance companies, big industries, public utilities,
and foreign trade; central planning of all productive
activities, including those of the private sector; a constitutional reform that was to include "a reform of the
parliamentary system destined to democratize its composition [*sic*] and increase its efficacy"; and the grant-
ing of official status to "neighborhood and resident
committees and other popular organizations in the
villages, towns, and city boroughs"; an anti-imperialist
and anticolonialist "independent foreign policy"; and
the "progressive establishment of closer links with the

Latin American nations, especially with the Republic of Cuba, in order to ensure mutual aid in the common struggle for our complete emancipation from imperialism."[28] It is evident that the authors of this platform had in mind a revolution similar to that carried out by Castro.

The friction that has arisen between the Chilean Communist leadership and the Cubans does not concern the Socialists, who are a purely national party and thus not pledged to defend the interests of the Soviet Union. There is no reason for them to become less sympathetic toward Cuba because the Communists' attitude toward that country has changed. Furthermore, in spite of their alliance, the Communists are still their competitors for the leadership of the Chilean Left. As the history of the Socialists shows, their natural inclination is to compete with the Communists "from the Left" by demonstrating that they are more radical and more loyal to the cause of the revolution. The Cuban issue gives them an opportunity to do so.

It is therefore not surprising that a strong pro-Chinese current now made its appearance within the Socialist Party of Chile. Characteristically the new trend became noticeable within a few weeks of the time when Espártaco Editores began making Spanish translations of Chinese ideological materials available to the Chilean public. Whereas in the Communist Party only a small group of ordinary members dared to declare for the Chinese, and, in the Secretary-General's words, "they were not able to split one single cell," in the Socialist Party the Chinese cause was espoused by the entire left wing.

[28] *El Siglo*, January 25, 1963.

It is easy to sneer at the amazing transition of the Chilean Socialists from anticommunism to Popular-Frontism to Peronism to Titoism to Castroism and later, at least partially, to Maoism. This seems to be the behavior of a political chameleon. But viewed in a more tolerant mood, it denotes an openmindedness, a curiosity, and an inclination to intellectual adventure that to this European observer at least are a great relief after the stuffiness, narrowmindedness, and obstinate anti-intellectualism of European social democracy. European socialism is characterized by a stubborn resistance to new ideas, an extreme reluctance to adapt itself to changing political and social conditions.[29] This certainly cannot be said of the Chilean Socialists.

The susceptibility of the Chilean Socialists to intellectual fashions does not mean that they are lacking in basic principles. If that were so, it would be impossible to explain the remarkable vitality of their party, its ability to recover from the schisms that have plagued it throughout its troubled history, and from the serious decline it suffered during the 1940's. Actually the various "isms" to which the Chilean Socialists have successively adhered have been little more than different labels used to cover a box containing one and the same set of concepts. These basic notions are

1. *Nationalism.* From the time of their first leader Marmaduke Grove onward the Chilean Socialists have always been fervent nationalists both in the narrower Chilean and in the wider Latin American sense.

2. *Antiparliamentarianism.* The Chilean Socialists

---

[29] See, among others, the history of the British Labour Party after World War II and the entire history of the German Social Democrats from Kautsky's 1898 defeat of Bernstein until after World War II.

regard the parliamentary system in an underdeveloped country like Chile as a device by which the oligarchy maintains itself in power, and they are extremely skeptical as to the possibility of implementing any radical change in the power structure within the framework of this system. Not being sectarians, they do not advocate abstention from voting; they do not refuse to participate in parliamentary activities or reject the very considerable material and political benefits accruing from this participation. But they do not want to cooperate with the established parties that are representative of the system, and indeed the experience of their one lapse from this principle, the Popular Front period, has taught them that it is fatal to the unity of the party to do so. Paradoxically the Communists are far more willing to operate within the limits of the parliamentary system and to collaborate with its representatives.

3. *Socialism.* This is of the utilitarian type so widespread among the nationalists of underdeveloped countries. The Chilean Socialists reject free enterprise because in their country it is synonymous with foreign investment and foreign domination of the economy. They hold that foreign capital is unwilling and domestic capital both unwilling and unable to implement the drastic program of industrialization that in their view is necessary in order to raise the living standard of the masses. They believe that the investment funds for this vast program can be raised and channeled into the right direction only by state planning and by state ownership of the basic means of production.

4. *Proletarianism.* The leadership of the Chilean Socialists, in contrast to that of the Communists, has

always been composed of intellectuals. But these intellectuals consider the proletariat, that is, the industrial and agricultural workers, to be the only political force capable of bringing about real changes in the Chilean power structure.

The Chilean Socialists may thus be defined as a nationalistic party of the Left, profoundly antioligarchical and basically antiparliamentarian, pledged to carry out radical changes in the political and economic system — changes they hope to achieve by using the industrial and agricultural workers as a striking force.[30]

An examination of the ideas of two of the party's leading ideologues will show that there is a real consistency in the party's basic thinking.

RAÚL AMPUERO

The Secretary-General of the Socialist Party of Chile, Senator Raúl Ampuero, was born in 1917 and is a youthful looking man. As a public speaker Ampuero conforms to the general Chilean pattern of oratorical drabness; in private conversation he has a captivating manner and a deceptively frank and candid way of answering questions. One rather wonders how such an apparently naïve man can hold his own in the rough

[30] The Socialist Party also has a small right wing bitterly opposed to the alliance with the Communists and regarded by some observers as being "social democratic" in the European sense. But the ideologist of this group, Julio César Jobet, author of *Los fundamentos del marxismo* (4th ed.; Santiago de Chile: Prensa Latinoamericana, 1964), is a rigidly doctrinaire Marxist-Leninist. The most prominent personality of the Socialist right wing is the highly respected Rector of the University of Chile, Eugenio González Rojas, a former party secretary and author of the 1949 party program.

and tumble of political life until one suddenly realizes that his rapid and seemingly spontaneous answers are the product of an exceptionally quick mind, and that he is always on his guard and careful never to say anything that may be used against him by his opponents outside or inside the party.

Ampuero is a highly competent professional, a machine politician of great experience and toughness, who has managed to maintain control over a turbulent and rebellious party ever since he pushed aside the old-guard leadership in 1946. Besides being a skillful and determined machine politician, Ampuero is one of the leading intellectual lights of the Socialist Party and one of its most interesting ideologists.

In an ideological debate that took place in March 1962 he proved to be more than a match for the collective brain power of the Communist leadership. That debate clearly delineated the differences between the Socialists, a purely Chilean party of the extreme Left, and the Communists, the Chilean branch of an international movement taking its cue from Moscow and pledged to unconditional support of Soviet foreign policy. Moreover it demonstrated that the official opinion of the Chilean Socialists, in spite of their differences with the Communists, is far to the left of that of the member parties of the Socialist International.

The debate was sparked by certain statements made by Ampuero in the course of an interview broadcast by a local radio station in the far south of Chile and retransmitted, perhaps against his intentions, by the radio stations of the capital. Since these statements were highly critical of Soviet foreign policy and of some fundamental tenets held by the Chilean Communists, they were attacked by Politburo member Orlando Millas in an article published by the Communist daily newspaper *El Siglo*. Millas complained that the tone of Ampuero's statements had been "intransigent" and that, although it might not be quite correct to classify them as anticommunist, they were couched in unfriendly terms pleasing to "the reactionaries."[31]

Ampuero countered with a long statement to *El Siglo*, in which he not only maintained his original position but also considerably amplified his criticism of communist ideological tenets and Soviet policies. What had hitherto ostensibly been a debate between individuals was then raised to the party level by an open letter signed by Luis Corvalán in his capacity as Secretary-General and spokesman for the Politburo of the Communist Party. The letter was couched in conciliatory terms and, while maintaining Millas' objections to Ampuero's views, stressed that the Communists did not desire to impose their views on their allies. However, Corvalán distinctly cracked the whip by pointing out that the Chilean revolutionary movement could ill afford to estrange the Soviet Union by dissenting from its foreign policy:

In order to carry forward its anti-imperialist, antifeudal, and ultimately socialist revolution the Chilean people and its future government need the support of the socialist world. Neither the solidarity of the Latin American nations nor the aid, if that were possible, of a country such as Yugoslavia will suffice. The collaboration of the whole of what you are pleased to define as the "so-called socialist

31 See Orlando Millas, "El senador Raúl Ampuero y los topicos anticomunistas," in *La polémica socialista-comunista*, published by the Central Committee of the Socialist Party (Santiago de Chile: Prensa Latinoamericana, S. A., [1962]), p. 5.

camp," and in the first place of the Soviet Union, will be indispensable. And it is logical to assume that this will be obtained on the basis of a correct attitude toward international problems.[32]

Far from being impressed, Ampuero further amplified his criticism in a second letter to *El Siglo*, which made it clear that any further Communist insistence on a change in the Socialist attitude could result only in a rupture of relations between the two parties. In order to avoid this, the Communists refrained from further open polemics. In public the Socialists thus had the last word. Discussions were continued in private and apparently resulted in a compromise favorable to the Socialists.

The main points made by Ampuero in this highly interesting public debate were:

1. Rejection of the principle of unified world leadership of the revolutionary movement under Soviet (or Chinese) control. In his original radio statement Ampuero had declared

We believe that every country and every nation must choose the road adequate to their specific circumstances in order to construct socialism. . . . That is why we have always enthusiastically applauded the attitude of the Yugoslav government and nation in defending their right to build socialism in the Yugoslav manner. For the same reason, behaving in the same way toward Albania as the Soviet Union behaved toward Yugoslavia constitutes a violation of the principle of national self-determination of the peoples, although we are absolutely not in agreement with the Albanian regime. In short, our attitude toward the present Russian and in the second place Chinese hegemony

[32] Luis Corvalán, in "Carta de la Comisión Política del Partido Comunista," *ibid.*, p. 34.

over the communist movement is one of criticism and of a freedom of judgment that we exercise whenever we can with all our energy and complete sincerity.[33]

In their reply the Communists insisted that they too accepted the principle that every nation should choose its own road to socialism. They then claimed that the Communist Party of the Soviet Union did not exercise ideological and political command functions in the communist world movement but only the function of "a directing center in the best sense of the word, a center as a vanguard of advanced ideas."[34]

Ampuero disposed of this argument by saying

There is no direction without subordination, no vanguard without a rearguard. . . . We sincerely believe that the decisions of the Chilean Communist Party are made in Chile by its own leaders. If that were not so, our alliance would be bereft of any moral foundation. But we also believe that the mentality of the communist parties, including that of the Chilean Communist Party, is still weighed down by a whole gamut of concepts, prejudices, and erroneous theoretical tenets whose persistence can be explained only by this acknowledgment of a special authority, the Soviet center. To cite a recent and dramatic example, on the validity of which you may agree, the entire Stalinist phase was accepted by the communist camp without the slightest criticism, whereas it was evident to any tolerably well-informed observer that over there the dictatorship of the proletariat was being replaced by a bureaucratic tyranny, and workers' democracy by a repulsive autocracy. It was precisely after the proclamation of the Soviet constitution of 1936 — the "most democratic in the world," according to the language of the period — that the phase described by Khrushchev as a period of unheard-of terror began, which

[33] Quoted by Millas in "El senador," *ibid.*, pp. 6 f.
[34] In "Carta de la Comisión Política del Partido Comunista," *ibid.*, p. 27.

started by seeking its victims among the Soviet Communist leaders themselves. . . .[35]

2. Rejection of the policy of military blocs and of the theory of the two camps. In his radio interview Ampuero declared

We reject the policy of military blocs. We believe that by engaging the countries of its orbit in the Warsaw Pact, by binding them with military agreements, by carrying out arbitrary actions in the military field, such as the latest atomic explosion, the Soviet Union is drawing the world into a form of struggle that is fundamentally military, whereas in our view each country bears in its own bosom the social forces that will facilitate a social transformation of its economic system.[36]

To this the Communists gave their stock answer: "The world is divided, one may say, into two main antagonistic camps, the capitalist camp and the socialist camp. . . . Capitalism, by its nature, is inclined toward war. Socialism, also by its nature, is inclined toward peace. . . ."[37]

Ampuero counterattacked:

For a consistent Marxist the world is not basically divided into two "camps," in the sense of two perfectly defined geographical areas, even though this fact is of undeniable importance in contemporary reality. . . . To claim that the "camp," i.e., a coalition of states, is the socialist element par excellence, and that more or less unconditional support of its policy determines the degree to which those struggling against the capitalist system are socialist, implies an erroneous and one-sided attitude with transcendent practical consequences. . . . It leads to subordination of the strategic

[35] In "Respuesta del Comité Central del Partido Socialista," *ibid.*, pp. 40 f.
[36] Quoted by Millas in "El senador," *ibid.*, p. 7.
[37] "Carta de la Comisión Política, *ibid.*, p. 21.

necessities of the workers' movement to the national security of the socialist states, to underestimation of every revolutionary victory that is not accompanied by integration into the system of the "camp," to evaluation of the political conquests of the peoples and of their parties in terms of their international commitments and not of their intrinsic value. . . .

We cannot deny the right of the Soviet bloc to maintain powerful armies, to organize its defense, to improve its military equipment. What we object to is the pre-eminence that these measures are acquiring in the international policy of the bloc, and the weight of this armed might in the internal relations of the alliance. . . . The forcible methods employed against the Hungarian insurrection, after ten years of Communist rule, may conform to considerations of military strategy but not to socialist methods of relations between nations. The methods of pressure bordering on military invasion that were employed against Yugoslavia after 1948 . . . constitute further proof of how specifically military concepts can replace any principled socialist policy within the bloc.[38]

3. Rejection of the Communists' claim to an ideological monopoly. Ampuero declared

The Communists . . . have traditionally displayed an attitude that we consider to be rather dogmatic, sectarian, in the sense that they suppose that Marxism and the specific historical conclusions that its ideologists have drawn in other periods are irrefutable, definite, and more or less eternal. That is also why in our party we have a freedom to criticize and an interplay of opinion that are much more lively and dynamic than what takes place in the Communist Party.[39]

4. Criticism of the Chilean Communists' policy of

38 In "Respuesta del Comité Central," *ibid.*, pp. 44 f.
39 Quoted by Millas in "El senador," *ibid.*, pp. 8 f.

the Peaceful Road. Ampuero criticized this policy "from the Left":

If the proclamation of the peaceful road were a mere confirmation of the readiness to exhaust all the electoral possibilities afforded by bourgeois democracy, this would be nothing new, and consequently there would be no justification for the emphasis now placed on this formula. In 1958 FRAP fought the election contest without speaking of its devotion to the peaceful road. The people's movement has always used all legal means whenever possible. But the *peaceful* character of the methods you now recommend appears to go farther than a mere decision to participate in an electoral contest: although this may not be your intention, it tends to give the masses a false confidence in what we may call the "normality" of the democratic institutions, in the impartial functioning of the representative mechanisms; whereas we, on the contrary, are convinced that in view of the intensity of the social crisis that we are now experiencing the entire formalism of the traditional republican system is being deceitfully infringed in order to perpetuate the rule of the oligarchic minorities. . . . If the very basis of the democratic contest is deliberately changed in order to impede the apparently inevitable victory of the people, then we can only preach: not peace, but resistance. That is why our decision to participate in the presidential election signifies at the same time — by every means within our reach — a *change* in the electoral norms. That is also why we do not confuse acceptance of the "electoral road" with sanctification of the "peaceful road" in the usual sense. . . .

No one has the right to entertain illusions as to the attitude of the reactionaries in the event of their defeat in 1964; some sectors might sincerely accept it, but others are already preparing to prevent it without any half measures. At present the Republican Militia[40] is being clandestinely

---

[40] A reference to attempts to build up a rightist paramilitary organization.

organized, and in the armed forces they are eliminating without inhibitions every officer who manifests a progressive mentality or, because of his disciplined attitude, is considered a danger to the perpetuation of the oligarchic system. In Ecuador, Brazil, and Argentina we have recently seen instances of how the Right interprets the sanctity of representative institutions and national sovereignty.

We too desire earnestly to avoid violence on our soil; revolutionaries never seek it motivated by a sort of political sadism, but we would disown our leading role and weaken the political consciousness of the people if we transformed our desire for internal peace into the substantial aim of our activity. By this we would only encourage those who seek to perpetuate their privileges by fire and sword.[41]

When the debate was finally concluded behind closed doors, an agreement was apparently reached to refrain from further polemics in the mass media such as radio and daily newspapers. But the Socialists evidently reserved their right to voice critical opinions of communism and the Soviet Union at Socialist Party functions — even when these were open to the general public — and in their theoretical publication *Arauco*.

Ampuero exercised that right in a highly interesting lecture in a Socialist Party public seminar in April 1963, which throws further light on his thinking.

He started out by drawing a clear line between the Chilean Socialists and the parties of the Socialist (or Second) International:

We classify as socialist only those regimes or movements that aim at the abolition of private ownership of the means of production and recognize the working class as the dynamic element par excellence in this change of the social structure. . . . This criterion eliminates from our consideration the totality of those parties of which today the Second

[41] *La polémica socialista-comunista, op. cit.*, pp. 53 ff.

International is composed and which in the course of the last years, in consequence of successive changes in their programs and ideologies, have ended by incorporating themselves more or less resolutely in the defense of the established capitalist order.[42]

He then stated that it would be futile to debate whether or not

communism, such as we know it, is or is not a manifestation of contemporary socialism. Any theoretical objection that might be formulated would run up against one indubitable fact: for the man of today, the citizen of the twentieth century, for contemporary public opinion, communism . . . is one of the concrete and historical manifestations of contemporary socialism. The reasons for this acceptance are rather obvious. The revolution of 1917 overthrew the feudal-capitalistic power of the old Russia and installed, indubitably, a new type of state and government . . . in which the participation of the peasants and the working class was evident and real.

This great experiment took place, however, under such unfavorable circumstances as economic backwardness and capitalist encirclement, which inevitably led to the establishment of rigid internal discipline under monopolistic party leadership:

Just as various socialist theoreticians of that day had feared, these objective elements and these tendencies were the germ of later deformations. . . . The numerical and qualitative power of the bureaucracy increased, its political influence spread wider, and economic management was centralized to an unheard-of extent. On the theoretical and the practical levels the role and the machinery of the state were strengthened, in contradiction to the predictions of the founders of socialism as to the role of the state after the

[42] This and the following quotations are from *Arauco*, No. 40, May 1963.

fall of capitalism. And in the same measure as these phenomena blossomed the masses were despoiled of any real
and direct participation in the management of the new
government and system. In the course of time the ruling
party itself was subjected to the repressive forces of the
state, to the police force, which at a certain moment came
to constitute the repressive and political organ of the ruling
bureaucratic caste.

This in brief characterizes what we know as "the Stalinist
era." From what we have said it also follows that this historical phenomenon and its monstrous characteristics cannot
be explained from the scientific Marxist viewpoint by a
simple reference to the so-called "personality cult." The
"personality cult" could be only the external form of a phenomenon that has much deeper roots in the sociological,
economic, and political development of the new Soviet
state. . . .

From this, Ampuero drew the conclusion:

The experience of Stalinism has shown the need for democratic institutional instruments in the workers' state in order
to neutralize the regressive tendencies that might originate
within its body.

Ampuero's cure for the evils of Stalinism was the
same one proposed by the Yugoslav Communists: the
so-called system of "workers' self-management":

It is debatable whether we have already arrived at the
highest forms of socialism by making the state the sole
property owner and assigning it as the natural representative of the working class. Judging by recent experience it
would seem that state property is still a long way from
really being property of the community, of society. And in
this sense the self-management of the means of production
and the development of democracy in the industrial and
economic field constitute important live approaches that
today are being implemented in varying degrees in some
states that have succeeded in abolishing capitalism.

Ampuero expressed the belief that the Yugoslavs have succeeded in establishing "direct democracy":

The Yugoslav comrades reserve this name for a system of relations among the citizen, the producer, and the state that is based on the commune as the living and vital cell of society that is extended to the social management of services and activities that ordinarily remain in the hands of the state as a governmental machine and ultimately transforms in the most complete manner the participation of the voter, the common and ordinary citizen, in public affairs. That is to say, there is a substantial difference between our Chilean voter, who gives a mandate to a deputy, senator, or president on one specific occasion and for a prolonged period, and the concept of the voter as an active factor of social development, participating in the selection of his representatives, in their election, in the supervision of their activity, and who even has the right to revoke their mandate.

Ampuero even accepted the Yugoslav form of the one-party system with the party as an elite group controlling a broader organization, the Socialist Alliance of the Working People of Yugoslavia, which it uses as a transmission belt. He approved of

the notion of a party as center, nucleus, and spinal column of a broader organization of institutions, movements, and individuals faithful to the revolutionary creed. There is evidently an important difference between the concept of the Bolshevik party as the exclusive and unique representative of the political opinion of the masses and certain new experiments now in process of formation or implementation. For the Yugoslav comrades the Socialist Alliance of the Working People constitutes an ample political and social platform from which the League of Communists receives many stimuli, and which at the very least gives it the means for an exact appraisal of the tendencies, inclinations, and aspirations of public opinion. . . .

In the July 1963 issue of *Arauco* Ampuero published an article on the Sino-Soviet dispute, which was the product of an inner-party debate with Clodomiro Almeyda, the leader of the pro-Chinese wing of the Socialist Party.

Ampuero considered the Sino-Soviet dispute as a positive event — not as a crisis of disintegration but as a starting point toward a "coherent reconstruction of the international revolutionary movement," namely, as a "revolutionary world bloc, much vaster and more flexible than the present communist movement," an "international democratic integration of the anticapitalist and anti-imperialist forces." Ampuero therefore rejected "the mere substitution of Soviet hegemony by Chinese hegemony," since "true internationalism does not permit ideological lines or strategic norms that are not the product of collective, multilateral, and democratic decisions by all the forces involved in the action."[43]

As for the specific issues of the dispute, Ampuero severely censured the Chinese for what he termed their "manifest underestimation" of the consequences of an atomic holocaust and for their assertion of an "alleged antagonism between socialism and peace."

He said that he advocated a true policy of peaceful coexistence, although he stressed that such a policy could not apply to relations between oppressed and oppressor nations. Furthermore a policy of coexistence between military blocs does not satisfy him: "Peaceful coexistence will develop all of its historic possibilities only where the old policy of blocs is definitively abandoned."

We thus see that Ampuero, while criticizing the

[43] These and the quotations that follow are from *Arauco*, No. 42, July 1963.

Chinese, by no means unconditionally supported the Soviet point of view. On one important issue he even sided with the Chinese: He wholeheartedly approved their statement that the vast regions of Asia, Africa, and Latin America are the "storm centers of world revolution." He did not agree with the Soviet thesis that the leading role in the alliance of revolutionary forces belongs to the "socialist world system," that is, to the countries of the Soviet bloc, who exercise a decisive influence on the course of the world revolution by the force of their example, by their economic successes. In Ampuero's opinion this thesis "exaggerates the stimulating influence" of Soviet economic successes on the underdeveloped world. He also pointed out that the level of individual well-being in the Soviet Union is still not as high as in the "imperialist countries," that is, in the Western democracies.

These quotations may suffice to give us a picture of Ampuero's ideological position. The leader of the Chilean Socialists certainly has little or nothing in common with a European social democrat. His feelings for social democracy, which "combines a progressive withdrawal from socialist goals with a complete inability to understand the importance and historical meaning of the struggle of the colonial and dependent countries," are not far removed from contempt. His objections to the communist slogan of "the Peaceful Road to power" clearly demonstrate that he is highly skeptical as to the possibility of carrying out substantial changes of the social structure within the framework of parliamentary institutions. Ampuero does not even believe that the existence of opposition parties is necessary in order to safeguard what he regards as democracy. The "direct democracy" in the economy and public administration on the Yugoslav pattern, which he favors so much, is perfectly compatible with highly authoritarian one-man rule. Ampuero is certainly far too intelligent for this fact to have escaped him during his visits to Yugoslavia.

Great as Ampuero's enthusiasm for Titoism may be, he is not a doctrinaire blindly copying the Yugoslav system and Yugoslav policy in every detail. Thus his attitude toward the Sino-Soviet conflict differs from that of the Yugoslavs, whose policy in this respect is far more favorable to the Soviet Union. He maintains an intermediate position.

We see that Ampuero modifies or tones down his Titoism wherever it might conflict with his position as a non-Communist and a Latin American nationalist. He is a Titoist because, and only so far as, this ideology is of use to him as the leader of a nationalistic party of the Left. He had been highly critical of the Soviet system and of Soviet foreign policy long before he became a Titoist; but Titoism has made it possible for him to differentiate his criticism from that voiced by the social democrats, whom he abhors.

At first glance Ampuero seems to be blindly espousing the foreign ideology of Titoism, but in reality he uses and adapts this ideology to his own, specifically Latin American aims. The ideological terminology is imported from abroad, but it is used to justify policies that are Latin American.

CLODOMIRO ALMEYDA

Clodomiro Almeyda was born in 1923. He is a practicing lawyer and a professor of social science at the University of Chile, has the same political background as Ampuero, but his personality is very different. Almeyda is not a leader of men nor is he able to manipulate a political machine, and he was easily outmaneuvered by Ampuero when he tried to marshal the forces of an inner-party opposition against the Secretary-General. But his cold, hard brilliance of mind and his gift of clear and concise expression make him one of the very few ideologists of note so far produced by a movement that has hitherto been remarkable more for the violence of its emotions than for lucidity of thought — Latin American extreme nationalism.

Almeyda's approach to political and ideological problems is the exact opposite to Ampuero's. He starts out from concrete Latin American phenomena and seems interested in general ideas only when they have a direct and visible bearing on Latin American reality. Yet all the ideas expressed in his writings fit together to form a completely consistent, tight-knit system of Latin American political philosophy. This is all the more remarkable in that most of his writing is journalistic, consisting of brief editorials written for the Socialist press. His book, *Reflexiones políticas,* containing a selection of these editorials dating back to the Ibáñez era of the 1950's, is so remarkable for its clarity of expression and precision of thought that it could well serve as a textbook for foreign students of Latin American nationalism.[44]

First and foremost, Almeyda is a Latin American

[44] My analysis of Almeyda's political philosophy is based on his book, *Reflexiones políticas* (Santiago de Chile: Prensa Latinoamericana, S. A., 1958); his 1957 lecture, *Visión sociológica de Chile,* published in Santiago de Chile by the Academia de las Escuelas de Ciencias Políticas y Administrativas, 1957; several essays in the Socialist ideological review *Arauco;* and some more recent editorials in the Socialist tabloid *Ultima Hora.*

nationalist. His nationalism is far more vehement than that of Raúl Ampuero. He is violently opposed to the United States. For him, North American "political, economic, and ideological penetration of our country, as of all Latin America, [is] a real peril . . . compromising our sovereignty, our culture, our way of life, our future, and our means of building a wealthier and more equitable community in accordance with our authentic needs."[45]

Yet for all his demagogic vituperation Almeyda is far too sophisticated a political thinker to regard "Yankee imperialism" as the root cause of the evils besetting Chile. He agrees with those students of Chilean history who, rightly or wrongly, believe that Chile's economic and cultural development was vitiated as early as the sixth and seventh decades of the nineteenth century — long before North American economic influence made itself felt.[46] Before this, living in relative cultural isolation, Chile had enjoyed several decades of political, military, and economic pre-eminence in Latin America. According to Almeyda the rot set in through contamination of the country's ruling class by European cultural influences:

The contact between our Chile, which had only just

[45] Almeyda, *Reflexiones políticas, op. cit.,* pp. 84 f.
[46] This is the thesis first developed by the Chilean historian Francisco A. Encina in 1912 in his book *Nuestra inferioridad económica: sus causas, sus consecuencias* (new ed.; Santiago de Chile: Editorial Universitaria, S. A., 1955). For Encina the fact that the lion's share of Chile's mineral wealth is foreign owned is not the cause but the result of what he terms his country's "economic inferiority." The economist Aníbal Pinto Santa Cruz, in his book *Chile, un caso de desarrollo frustrado* (Santiago de Chile: Editorial Universitaria, S. A., 1962), maintains that Chile's economic development took a wrong turn from the moment its government adopted the laissez-faire policies advocated by its economic adviser, the French economist Courcelle-Seneuil, who stayed in Chile from 1855 to 1863.

emerged from its colonial chrysalis, and the expansive, capitalist and bourgeois, free-trading and opulent Europe infected the country with patterns of life and behavior, with a mentality and an ideology imported from abroad, which in their places of origin were indeed the natural expression of social progress and thus played a positive role, but here in Chile were foreign products that had no rapport with our own rhythm of development and which, incorporated into our style of individual and communal life, produced very grave internal maladjustments and contradictions difficult to resolve. One may say that the country was afflicted with indigestion by these foreign foodstuffs. . . .[47]

This twentieth-century Socialist rejects many of the values of the Renaissance and Enlightenment with the rigor of a Grand Inquisitor:

A large part of the Chilean and Latin American leftist "intelligentsia" is still dominated by a foreign mentality, that is, one of unconditional adherence to nineteenth-century values and ideals that here on our continent are bereft of any historical reality and social efficacy. Parliamentary democracy, the party system, the cult of abstract liberty and democracy, etc. are still veritable idols that one must not criticize or at least must adapt to our conditions of life. . . . Eternal and infallible Reason was nothing but the historical instrument used by the European bourgeoisie to carry out its revolution in the conditions prevailing over there. Our road to economic liberation, political development, and cultural blossoming takes another direction and demands other values. . . .[48]

Again and again Almeyda stresses his main theme, that European standards are not applicable to Latin America and the other underdeveloped areas of the world:

. . . Nationalism, which in decomposing supercapitalistic

47 Almeyda, *Visión sociológica de Chile, op. cit.*, pp. 8 f.
48 Almeyda, *Reflexiones políticas, op. cit.*, p. 16.

states is a synonym for oppression and colonialism, assumes a progressive, liberating, and even revolutionary aspect in the dependent countries. Authoritarianism, which in the typical capitalist countries is the weapon employed to destroy the workers' movement, in dependent countries happens to be the only way to organize the community and to mobilize the productive forces against feudalism and the ruling oligarchies. Democratic liberalism, on the other hand, which in advanced capitalist countries permits the development of the people's movement, in the dependent countries only serves to anarchize society and to facilitate the rule of the reactionary minorities under cover of a semblance of public liberties that does not reach the masses and that they are unable to use.[49]

Almeyda believes that democracy has led Chile to a stalemate:

Side by side with the latifundia, which in the main are still intact, there coexist the big highly productive mining enterprises producing for the metropolis and foreign to our national economy; and the unstable native industry asphyxiated by the narrowness of the market and generally equipped with superannuated machinery, with a strong tendency toward monopoly. A permanently expanding, service-providing middle class and a working class with a relatively mature and influential political and syndical organization complete the picture of this many-sided sociological panorama, within which all these forms of existence aspire to coexist without destroying each other, lubricated by the daily experience of a democratic political activity as formalistic as it is sterile, which covers up the basic fact that there does not exist a veritable political authority able to resolve the social contradictions and conflicts in one sense or the other.[50]

At one time Almeyda hoped that the Ibáñez move-

[49] *Ibid.*, pp. 58 f.
[50] Almeyda, *Visión sociológica de Chile, op. cit.*, pp. 20 f.

ment would provide the authority strong enough to break the social stalemate. In a comment on Ibáñez' triumph in the 1952 presidential election he wrote

The Chilean people . . . understood that in order to put an end to economic chaos and social anarchy it was necessary that a strong and purposeful authority should rule and be obeyed. And it desired the mission of this authority to be the definite inclination of the scales toward the people, thus deciding the social struggles in favor of labor, of the masses, and of the native majority. This was the essential significance of the Ibáñez candidacy, which, being essentially popular, did not use the traditional libertarian and democratistic language of the petty-bourgeois politician but revolved around the necessity of at last providing Chile with a strong government that would represent and organize the scattered progressive social forces.[51]

Being one of Ibáñez' most enthusiastic Socialist supporters, Almeyda joined his cabinet, serving first as Minister of Labor (from December 1952 to March 1953) and later as Minister for the Mining Industry (from June to October 1953).[52] Three years later, though disillusioned with Ibáñez, Almeyda still defended him against the efforts of the democratic parties to curb his powers by a constitutional change from the presidential system to pure parliamentarianism:

We cannot and must not desire that in replacement of the present system of government the retrogressive interests of feudalism, of imperialism, of the parasitic middle class, of clericalism, and of the politicians take possession of Chile under the mask of a parliamentarian and party government, which is what our oligarchic and aristocratic clique has always wanted to install.[53]

[51] Almeyda, *Reflexiones políticas, op. cit.,* p. 71.
[52] See Würth Rojas, *op. cit.,* p. 358.
[53] Almeyda, *Reflexiones políticas, op. cit.,* p. 87.

It is interesting to note that the Chilean Communists took the diametrically opposed line. "The moment has come," said Communist Secretary-General Galo González in 1956,

> to put an end to the presidential regime. In essence this is a reactionary, absolutistic system of government. In our country it has been carried to such extremes that the president of the republic has come to be a veritable dictator. . . . All this runs counter to democracy and enables the government to act in disregard of parliament, the parties, and the organs of public opinion.[54]

The Communists therefore proposed to replace presidential supremacy by that of "a single-chamber parliament." Of course they were well aware that this formula, which meant elimination of the Senate, was unacceptable to the democratic parties. The purpose of the formula would appear to have been to enable them to support these parties in curbing presidential power without appearing merely to be hanging on to their coattails.

It goes without saying that so fervent an antiparliamentarian as Almeyda was strongly attracted to Peronism — although he was by no means blind to the defects of its leaders:

> The new energies and social forces released by the revolutionary process in Argentina since 1943 — indisputably a consequence of Peronism — are still in ebullition. The active appearance of the masses and of labor as the prime political force of their country, which is economically the most advanced in Latin America, has created unsuspected prospects of social evolution. It is true that the servile attitude

[54] *El Partido Comunista de Chile y el movimiento comunista internacional: documentos e informes emanados de plenos y congresos del Partido Comunista de Chile* (Santiago de Chile: Empresa Horizonte, [1964]), pp. 11 f.

of the labor unions toward government paternalism impairs the dignity and independence of the labor movement, and that, measured by Chilean standards, the level of political education of its leaders appears monstrously mediocre, but the importance of these negative and restrictive aspects palls beside the significance of the central fact that the Argentinian people today are present and active in the history of their country.[55]

After Perón had been deposed, Almeyda wrote an article harshly criticizing the Argentinian Socialists for having cooperated with the democratic parties in engineering the dictator's downfall:

Argentinian socialism was not a product of Argentinian social evolution. It was a product transplanted from Europe to Buenos Aires that came here with European immigrants, who wanted to perpetuate on American soil the patterns of thinking and behavior of European early twentieth-century social democracy. . . . The ideas and concepts by which it was animated were those that animated the European socialists of Jacobin and petty-bourgeois origin, for whom the French Revolution is still the culminating moment of history in which liberty, equality, and fraternity destroyed forever the reign of tyranny, ignorance, and oppression.

Our American people, the authentic one, not the one that is schooled in the universities, belongs to Masonic lodges, and reads French, has never understood this language. . . .

Argentinian socialism was never concerned with this common man. It never understood his feelings or his real needs. And when the Perón movement, for reasons of its own, toppled the oligarchy from its throne, gave social status to the worker, and allowed him to take possession of the streets, to speak out loud and strong, then he felt for the first time that now there was democracy and equality. . . .

The Argentinian Socialists never understood this. . . .

[55] Almeyda, *Reflexiones políticas, op. cit.,* p. 34.

This was one of the causes of the Argentinian Socialists' failure: their inability to see reality and the people such as it is and as it lives, without blinkers and deforming lenses. . . .

We Chilean Socialists must draw our conclusions from this experience and learn to find the authentic and real inspiration of our actions and our political philosophy in the harsh and unavoidable facts that shape our country and our people and determine our future.[56]

This indictment of a social democratic party for its courageous struggle against a dictatorship is certainly highly unfair. Yet it is one of the harsh and unavoidable facts of Latin American political life that the Argentinian Socialists, who were a party of some importance before the advent of Perón, have dwindled to a cluster of tiny sects whose influence is negligible. And it can also scarcely be denied that the reason for this decline is precisely the one indicated by Almeyda: their cooperation with the traditional democratic parties against the popular hero Perón.

The essays, newspaper articles, and lecture from which the foregoing quotations were culled were all written in the 1950's, a period in which Almeyda was greatly attracted by the authoritarianism of Perón and Ibáñez. Since then these influences have been replaced in his mind by those of Castro and Mao. Nevertheless Almeyda's latest writings show that basically his way of thinking has not changed. This is clearly demonstrated by his attitude toward President Illía of Argentina, a representative of the Radicals, one of the old established parties of that country.

In spite of the fact that Illía annulled the oil contracts

---

[56] *Ibid.*, pp. 48–50.

that one of his predecessors had accorded to North American oil companies, Almeyda considers him and his party to be part of "the anachronistic, semicolonial" political structure of Argentina:

His party is that of the old middle class, which did not understand the phenomenon of Peronism, never attempted to promote industrial development, and is still steeped in ancient and superannuated nineteenth-century values. . . . He and his party are far from promoting or even thinking of an authentic anti-imperialist and progressive policy. . . . Illía does not even know where he is going or why he does what he is doing. In spite of outward appearances his election means that Argentina has retrogressed from Perón.[57]

Whether in Peronist or Maoist guise, Almeyda remains true to himself. He is always basically the same authoritarian Latin American nationalist — a true representative of what Robert J. Alexander calls the "Jacobin Left," although he himself, with his dislike of the French Revolution, would certainly resent the epithet. It is Almeyda's nationalism and anti-imperialism that have drawn him into the Chinese camp. To him the essential aspect of the Chinese Communists' position, and the one that most appeals to him, is their stress on the importance of the "national liberation movement" of the underdeveloped areas as the decisive element in the struggle between socialism and capitalism.[58]

Almeyda's reasons for preferring the Chinese position to that of the Soviets are not dogmatic but purely practical and pragmatic. He does not favor the Chinese because they are more revolutionary per se, or more in accordance with the Marxist scriptures, which he rarely

[57] *Ultima Hora,* December 27, 1963.
[58] Statement to the author on December 22, 1963.

or never quotes in his writings, but because to him their theses make more sense from the point of view of the revolutionary movement of the underdeveloped areas.

In his lecture to the Socialist Party seminar in April 1963[59] Almeyda pointed out that the Chinese do not deny the possibility of avoiding a world war and are far from advocating such a war. But he stresses that the Chinese, in contrast to the Soviets, believe that the danger of war can be definitely eliminated only by the destruction of imperialism, so that the struggle for peace

is directly amalgamated with the struggle against imperialism. And the attack must be directed against the weakest flank. Imperialism is at its weakest, according to the Chinese thesis, on the front maintained by the national liberation movements, by the semicolonial and colonial peoples of the world. . . .

It seems to me that for the semicolonial and dependent countries, and especially for their revolutionary movement, a policy of peaceful coexistence, systematically implemented in the manner advocated by its most determined partisans, implies a position of subordination and passivity that appears to me to be negative. . . . Furthermore it seems to me . . . that there is a certain correspondence between the policy of peaceful coexistence between states of different social structure and the internal policy of the peaceful road in the semicolonial and dependent countries. . . . And for the following reason: If the semicolonial countries base their policies on the assumption that the fate of socialism will be decided in the economic competition between the Soviet Union and the United States, then they would naturally compromise the favorable development of this competition if they conducted, in their own territorial sphere, an aggressive policy against imperialism

[59] *Arauco*, No. 42, July 1963.

that might spark off a gigantic world conflict liable to destroy the economic gains of the socialist countries. . . .

It is interesting to note that Almeyda does not condemn the Soviets for their point of view, although he cannot share it. Their reasoning

is that of a country that is already on a relatively advanced level of socialist construction. But this reasoning does not apply to the black nations of Africa and the exploited nations of Asia, for whom that phrase of the Communist Manifesto is still completely valid: These are nations that have nothing to lose and everything to gain by revolution.

Almeyda admits that the policy of Peaceful Coexistence is in accordance with the national interest of the Soviet Union and does not blame the Soviets for pursuing it. Even though siding with the Chinese, he thus contrives to be milder in his judgment of Soviet policy than Ampuero. It would therefore be an impermissible simplification to interpret the division in the Socialist Party of Chile as being between the partisans of Moscow and those of Peking. It is between those who want to stay out of the conflict altogether and those who want to take the side of the Chinese. The former view is clearly expressed in the draft thesis on international affairs that Ampuero submitted to the Socialist Party congress in February 1964:

If Chilean socialism has from the beginning managed to avoid submission to the narrow and rigid structure of the communist movement . . . it would commit an irreparable error by now . . . taking part in a dispute that is convincing proof of the crisis of a decrepit machine.[60]

[60] Draft thesis on international politics, mimeographed sheet, February 1964; also published in *El Siglo*.

AMPUERO VERSUS ALMEYDA

In the light of their writings the differences between Ampuero and Almeyda appear to be slight. They agree in rejecting the Soviet thesis that the development of the Soviet economy is more important than "the national liberation struggle of the colonial and dependent countries." On paper Ampuero also concurs with Almeyda in condemning the communist slogan of the Peaceful Road.

But in practice, that is, in the case of the 1964 presidential election campaign, Ampuero tacitly accepted the Communist nonviolent strategy of keeping the campaign within the bounds of "bourgeois legality." It was mainly on this issue that Almeyda decided to give battle at the Socialist Party's national congress that was scheduled to open on February 13, 1964 in the important provincial city of Concepción. His forces were considerable: the key central Santiago regional organization, traditionally leftist and influenced by Trotskyism; the leadership of the Socialist Youth; several provincial organizations, including that of Concepción; and a number of trade-union representatives. The parliamentary delegation was split. If he cared to use it, Almeyda also had the support of the party's mass circulation daily newspaper, the afternoon tabloid *Ultima Hora.*

However, Almeyda's freedom of movement was hampered by the fact that the campaign for a parliamentary by-election of great, perhaps even decisive, importance for FRAP was in full swing. To provoke a leadership crisis at such a moment would have laid him open to the charge of sabotaging both the by-election and the presidential campaign chances of the "people's movement." An attempt to have the party congress postponed until after the by-election failed.

On January 11, 1964 the Central Santiago regional party congress met to elect the delegates for the national congress, and it was a foregone conclusion that these would be supporters of the Almeyda line.

It was at this point that Ampuero moved against his opponent. Emissaries of the party's Central Committee, which was completely under his control, arrived at the regional congress to announce that the election was annulled. In protest, Almeyda resigned from the post of regional secretary — probably a serious tactical mistake. Later a new regional congress was staged at Central Committee headquarters under Ampuero's personal supervision. It resulted in the election of a slate of delegates loyal to the Secretary-General.[61] Similar moves appear to have been made in the city of Concepción and in other provincial centers. A safe majority for Ampuero at the national congress was thus assured. His line triumphed without difficulty, and he was re-elected for a new term as Secretary-General.

The proceedings of the congress were secret, but Secretary-General Ampuero's main speech was later published.[62] It is a remarkable document, demonstrating the Secretary-General's ruthless determination to eliminate all organized opposition by applying the communist formula of Democratic Centralism. Ampuero denied the regional organizations of the party the right to a free choice of their delegates to the national party congress:

[61] *El Mercurio* and *Diario Ilustrado*, both of January 28, 1964.

[62] In *Arauco*, No. 49, February 1964. The following quotations are from Ampuero's speech in this issue of *Arauco*.

Is the party really a nationwide community or only a federation of local and regional groupings? If the latter were the case, it would be possible for each territorial unit to enjoy autonomy in nominating its representatives to the national congresses, subject only to elementary norms established in the Statutes. . . .

But the party is not a coalition of independent parishes; it is a unified and national instrument. The regions are geographical units integrated in an indivisible whole. What a regional committee accomplishes within its territorial limits is not uniquely its own concern, but it also interests and affects all other regional committees and the entire party.

The supreme authority of the National Organizational Commission represents this common interest and guarantees the national unity of the party.

This is the very essence of the communist organizational principle of Democratic Centralism, namely, that the central party authority controls the nomination of the delegates who are to elect its successor. But Ampuero went even further: He proclaimed allegiance to the communist principle of totalitarian party discipline:

But in order that the cycle: free discussion — democratic decision — disciplined execution be fully realized, it is not enough to establish ever more highly developed mechanisms. The principle of Democratic Centralism also implies a subjective element of capital importance: firm loyalty to the party, ideological identification with its line, its methods, its aims, and its destiny. . . . Mere adhesion to Marxist principles is not enough. . . . Only the everyday conduct of the member can furnish the elements for an evaluation of his loyalty. If he debates in an objective and clean manner, if he honestly respects the decisions and makes an authentic effort to assimilate them when he cannot agree with them, if he fulfills the concrete tasks with revolutionary discipline, then we cannot doubt his innermost identification with the party. On the other hand, he who employs incorrect procedures in order to prevail in the debates, resists and distorts democratic decisions, or avoids the fulfillment of activities that are necessary for the execution of a line with which he does not agree, is an element of disintegration. . . .

What Ampuero had in mind in speaking of "incorrect procedures in order to prevail in the debates" was organized opposition to the party leadership, or, as he called it, strictly in accordance with communist terminology, "factional activity":

In practice, the real threat to unity is constituted by factional activities, that is, when several members unite to work together, creating a clandestine machine within the official organization. The mere fact of promoting such a group indicates contempt for normal procedures and institutions and, in essence, for the party itself. . . .

In this utterly Stalinist speech he noted that even Trotskyism reared its ugly head in order to form "antiparty factions":

The party has always been extremely open-minded in accepting individuals and groups with a Trotskyist background. Such elements — heretics to the communist mind — would be objectionable to us only because of their sectarian inclinations, and above all because of their doubtful loyalty to the organization, in the double sense both of discipline and of their ability to correctly assimilate the socialist principles. We have had them of all kinds: some who managed to adapt themselves fully to our practices and orientation, but also others who sought refuge here in order to exploit our bases as a recruiting field for their own ends. . . .

The hour has come to separate the straw from the grain. If the party wants to become the authentic vanguard of the people's movement, it needs to put an end to the diversionist activities of the antiparty factions.

Ampuero accused the leftist opposition of aiming to create a "third workers' party":

In the main it is the Sino-Soviet conflict, but also the magic spell of the guerrilla activities in other countries or the irresponsible demagoguery of some adventurers, that constitute the basic platform of those who are attempting to form a new political grouping in rivalry to the Socialists and Communists. We would not have anything against this if they were content to recruit their followers by fair methods, openly competing with us, but this is not the case. Their expectations are based on the previous destruction of the Socialist Party. And although nobody is compelled to ask our permission to form a new party, we shall also not allow anybody to realize his objective by passively tolerating the disintegration of our own party.

The speech did not mean that the Socialist Party of Chile was on its way to becoming the replica of a totalitarian bolshevik machine. That would have been entirely against its tradition. It is unlikely that Ampuero seriously contemplated the bolshevization of his party, and if he had attempted such a change, he would certainly have failed. There was no mass purge of dissidents, and after the February 1964 congress the party remained ideologically as heterogeneous as before. It is also true that Ampuero's claim that there was a Trotskyist plot to destroy the Socialist Party was not entirely unfounded. The minute Trotskyist groups of the ultra-left were incessantly proclaiming the need for a third workers' party to be built on the remnants of the Communist and Socialist parties, who had allegedly become "revisionists" and "reformists." These people undoubtedly had their allies within the Socialist Party, notably in Almeyda's Santiago regional organization. Clodomiro Almeyda himself, the leader of the abortive revolt against Ampuero, was no Trotskyist and had an unblemished record of loyalty to the party, but he had to rely on the support of Trotskyist elements of whom the same could not be said.

In his debate with the Communists in 1962 Ampuero had claimed that "in our party we have a freedom to criticize and an interplay of opinion that is much more lively and dynamic than what takes place in the Communist Party."[63] Yet as soon as he was faced with something more serious than mere "interplay of opinion," namely, with a concerted attempt to change the party's leadership and political line, he had to resort to the totalitarian communist technique of Democratic Centralism and to justify his ruthless crushing of the opposition by an appeal to the totalitarian communist mystique of party discipline. This was the inevitable consequence of his own and his whole party's contempt for the procedures of parliamentary democracy. A political party cannot proclaim the democratic institutions of the state to be mere "fetishes" and a mere "mask to disguise the sordidness of the techniques of exploitation of the many by the few"[64] and at the same time practice democracy in its own inner-party life.

The FRAP presidential candidate, Socialist Senator Salvador Allende, played no active part in the proceedings of the party congress. Although popular in the party, his position was weak because he had no organ-

[63] Quoted by Millas in "El senador," *La polémica socialista-comunista, op. cit.,* p. 9.

[64] See the editorial in the same issue of the Socialist Party organ *Arauco* in which Ampuero's congress speech was printed (No. 49, February 1964). This editorial, entitled "Fetishes of Democracy," also claimed that "the defense of the democratic regime constitutes a play of words without meaning and without reality in social life."

ized following. He was no friend of Ampuero's and was known to have personal, though perhaps not doctrinal, sympathies for Havana and Peking. But he could not throw his weight on the scales in favor of Almeyda because this would have estranged him from the Communists, on whose assistance he had to rely in his presidential campaign.

For a strange, and as their opponents would have it, unholy, alliance had come about between the Communists and the Titoist Ampuero, whose influence they had previously regarded as nefarious. On the eve of the Socialist's party congress the Communist Party organ *El Siglo* printed the full text of Ampuero's congress theses on foreign policy in spite of the fact that these contained a condemnation of Soviet as well as capitalist bloc policies and even a proclamation of neutrality in the Sino-Soviet conflict. Although these views were of course highly heretical in Communist eyes, the Communists still preferred them to those of Almeyda, who insisted that the Chilean Socialists should consider themselves as belonging to the socialist world — but on the Chinese side.

The Communist press was jubilant when Ampuero triumphed at the Socialist congress. Ampuero's press conference after the congress was reported in *El Siglo* with banner headlines across the entire width of the front page, and the Communist mass circulation weekly *Vistazo*[65] waxed enthusiastic about his description of the ultraleftist opponents of the FRAP "peaceful" election campaign strategy as "soda-fountain guerrillas."

It is indicative of the weakness of the Communists'

[65] *Vistazo*, February 25, 1964.

position, and must have given them very uneasy feelings indeed, that they now had to applaud the victory and rely on the support of the man who had contemptuously referred to the crisis in their beloved international communist movement as "the crisis of a decrepit machine."

5

THE CHRISTIAN DEMOCRATIC ALTERNATIVE

OLIGARCHS AND JESUITS

As has already been emphasized, the use of European terminology and European ideologies by Latin American political parties is a source of serious error and confusion. This also applies in the case of the Chilean Christian Democrats. The Christian Democratic parties of Europe are coalitions of the most varied social elements, ranging from organized labor to sectors of the financial, industrial, and agrarian oligarchy. The Chilean Christian Democratic Party does not include the oligarchic element. Its position on the political spectrum is far to the left of that of the European Christian democrats.[1]

[1] The president of the Conservative Party, Francisco Bulnes Sanfuentes, relates that when the German Christian Democratic leader Gerstenmaier visited Chile, he told him: "I am a conservative. Ninety per cent of my party are conservatives, like the Conservative Party of Chile, and only ten per cent hold opinions similar to those expressed to me by some Christian Democratic deputies in this coun-

Yet this decidedly antioligarchic, left-of-center movement was originally the youth organization of the Conservative Party, one of the political groups representing the interests of the financial and agrarian oligarchy. The young men who in 1935 founded the Movimiento Nacional de la Juventud Conservadora, also called the Falange Nacional, did not intend to break with the oligarchic party leaders. They wanted only to revitalize the party and to increase its popular appeal. But in order to do so they advocated policies that threatened the interests of the oligarchy and profoundly antagonized the party leadership.

Laissez-faire Manchester liberalism in its most extreme form had been the economic doctrine of the Conservative Party since the middle of the nineteenth century, when it had been brought to Chile by the French economist Courcelle-Seneuil. But being the party of the Catholic Church, the Conservatives also paid lip service to the social doctrine of the encyclical Rerum novarum, which Pope Leo XIII had published in 1891. At first they did their best to ignore the flagrant contradiction between this encyclical and the economic doctrine of untrammeled individualism that guided their practical policies. But in the second and third decades of the twentieth century, two stubborn Chilean Jesuits, Fernando Vives del Solar and Jorge Fernández Pradel, took up the issue. They founded labor unions and credit, housing, and consumers' cooperatives and at the same time spread Catholic social doctrine among

try. It seems very strange to me that they, and not you, take part in international Christian Democratic congresses." Interview with Francisco Bulnes in Sergio Giulisasti Tagle, *Partidos políticos chilenos* (2nd ed., enlarged; Santiago de Chile: Editorial Nascimento, 1964), pp. 50 f.

the students of Santiago's Catholic University. Fernández Pradel conducted a study circle in which the future intellectual leaders of Chilean Catholicism were introduced to the literature of the French and Belgian Christian Social movements.

Complaints that Conservative Party leaders made to Father Vives' superiors about his allegedly subversive activities resulted in his being exiled for several prolonged terms to Argentina and Spain. Returning home to Chile in 1931 after an absence of fourteen years, the unrepentant Vives founded the Liga Social, an association of Catholic trade-union leaders and young intellectuals that had definite leftist, syndicalist tendencies. Some months before his death in 1935 he scandalized Catholic public opinion for the last time by declaring that

> Right and Left are not distinctions pertinent to the religious sphere; they are economic tendencies: the Rightists being the defenders of the system of the past, and the Leftists the protagonists of a new order.[2]

In the 1940's Vives' work was continued by his friend and disciple Alberto Hurtado Cruchaga, who founded a Catholic trade-union center, Acción Sindical y Económica de Chile; the periodical *Mensaje,* dedicated to the dissemination of Christian social ideas among the Catholic intelligentsia; and the Hogar de Cristo, a vast organization to provide food and shelter for the destitute. The spirit in which he conducted this work is revealed by his reply to the question whether the vagrants whom he helped were at least grateful: "Grateful for what? Have we the right to demand gratitude

2 Alejandro Magnet, *El Padre Hurtado* (Santiago de Chile: Editorial Del Pacífico, S. A., 1954), p. 156.

for taking a human being out of the filth in which we have forced him to live?"[3]

Although these Jesuits were not directly involved in the foundation and organization of the new left-of-center Catholic party, and Father Vives even had his clashes with the founders, they created the climate and the specific conditions that made its emergence possible. They were largely responsible for the severance of the close ties between the Church and the Conservative Party, a separation that Father Vives believed was imperative. In 1922, impelled by the desire to avoid a clash between the Church and the new left-of-center government of President Arturo Alessandri, the Primate of Chile, Archbishop Crescente Errázuriz of Santiago, had declared that "the Church is not responsible for the actions of any political party, nor does it attempt to influence them, leaving them completely independent." In the same pastoral letter the Archbishop decreed that "it is most strictly prohibited for any clergyman to act as the representative or agent of a political party." This declaration of neutrality was bitterly resented by the majority of the episcopate; and in 1933, after Archbishop Errázuriz' death, the bishops resolved to re-establish formal ties with the Conservative Party by declaring militancy in this body as obligatory for all Catholics. According to Alejandro Magnet,[4] Vives' influence was decisive in obtaining the letter from the Vatican Secretary of State, Cardinal Pacelli (later Pope Pius XII), by which the bishops' maneuver was blocked. Cardinal Pacelli settled the matter once and for all by reiterating the prohibition of party activities by clergy-

---

[3] *Ibid.*, p. 348.
[4] *Ibid.*, p. 155.

men and by again stressing that no political party could claim the right to exclusive representation of the Catholics.[5]

Thus by disseminating the doctrines of Rerum novarum and Quadragesimo anno[6] the Jesuits, together with a handful of allies among the Chilean clergy, laid the ideological foundations for a new basically Catholic party of far greater popular appeal than the Conservative Party.

THE FALANGE NACIONAL

The actual founders of the new party were a group of young Catholic intellectuals, alumni of the Catholic University of Santiago, one of the main centers of Father Fernández Pradel's and Father Vives' activities. The group participated in the students' demonstrations that led to the collapse of the Ibáñez dictatorship in July 1931 and was thereupon recruited into the Conservative Party by the party leader, Rafael Luis Gumucio, who had been one of the dictator's most determined opponents.

In 1934 two members of the group, Eduardo Frei and Manuel Garretón, traveled to Europe in order to attend a students' congress in Rome and also visited Spain, France, and Belgium. The influence of both Italian and Spanish fascism was reflected in the ideol-

[5] See Alejandro Silva Bascuñán, *Una experiencia Social Cristiana* (Santiago de Chile: Editorial Del Pacífico, S. A., 1949), pp. 37 ff.

[6] When the encyclical Quadragesimo anno was issued in 1931, the Conservative Party newspaper *Diario Ilustrado* refused to publish it. Father Fernández Pradel thereupon read salient passages from the encyclical in a radio broadcast. This caused Conservative Party dignitaries to lodge a complaint against him with his superiors, demanding his removal from the country. See Magnet, *op. cit.*, p. 151.

ogy and organizational pattern of the Conservative Youth Movement founded by the group in 1935. The stated aim of the Movimiento Nacional de la Juventud Conservadora was the organization of Chile's social and political institutions along the lines of the corporate state,[7] and in accordance with the latest European fashions it acquired a paramilitary branch, which was given the name Falange Nacional.

In the ideological luggage that Frei and Garretón brought back from Europe there were also, however, some very different and directly opposed concepts — the profoundly humanistic and democratic ideas of the French philosopher Jacques Maritain, whose lectures they had attended in Paris. Thirty years later Eduardo Frei and his collaborator Ismael Bustos published a booklet in which they summed up those aspects of Maritain's political philosophy that they considered to be of particular relevance to Chile. The authors pointed to his emphasis on the importance of pluralism in the modern world, namely on the need to "permit the co-existence of men belonging to different religious creeds in the bosom of one and the same civilization."[8] They further noted that for Maritain "democracy in its essence is only the secular name of the Christian ideal. . . . Maritain's philosophy thus closely links the democratic ideal with the evangelical message."[9] And finally the authors pointed to Maritain's belief that our age is a period of transition in which it is the duty of Christians to work for

---

[7] See Silva Bascuñán, *op. cit.*, pp. 56 f.

[8] Eduardo Frei and Ismael Bustos, *Maritain entre nosostros* (Santiago de Chile: Instituto de Educación Política, 1964), p. 17.

[9] *Ibid.*, p. 18.

the substitution of the inhuman system now visibly on its deathbed by a new system of civilization characterized by an integral humanism . . . [that] does not worship man but truly and effectively respects human dignity.[10]

Maritain had not yet fully expounded his political philosophy in the 1930's, but its humanistic and democratic nature was already abundantly clear. Furthermore his political opinions were known to be those of a democrat and antifascist: He actively opposed the French fascist movement of Charles Maurras, protested against Mussolini's invasion of Abyssinia, and caused an uproar in the Catholic world by denying that Franco's war against the Spanish Republic was a holy war against communist atheism in defense of religion.

Anyone not familiar with the specific political problems and intellectual atmosphere of Latin America will find it utterly incomprehensible that admiration for Mussolini's corporate state or for José Antonio Primo de Rivera's Spanish Falange could coexist in the same minds with admiration for Maritain. A brief examination of Eduardo Frei's first book, *Chile desconocido* (Unknown Chile),[11] published in 1937, will perhaps make this easier to understand.

This book, written by a young man of twenty-six, is a somewhat sketchy panorama of the political and social conditions prevailing in Chile in the mid-1930's, a few years after the collapse of the Ibáñez dictatorship and the re-establishment of democracy. Little was new and original in the author's analysis; it was clearly inspired by the two books that have been decisive in

[10] *Ibid.*, p. 54.
[11] Eduardo Frei, *Chile desconocido* (Santiago de Chile: Ediciones Ercilla, 1937).

forming the contemporary Chilean intellectual's picture of his country: Francisco Encina's *Nuestra inferioridad económica* and Alberto Edwards Vives' *La fronda aristocrática.*[12] Frei followed Encina and Edwards in describing the Chilean middle class as economically unproductive and politically inept — a verdict that later events proved to be far too severe. The influence of Edwards, who was an apologist of the Ibáñez dictatorship, is clearly visible in Frei's surprisingly positive view of the Ibáñez regime, which only a few years earlier he and his fellow students had helped to overthrow. And again in accordance with Encina, he largely blamed the deficiencies of Chile's educational system for her political and economic ills, though for opposite reasons: For Encina, Chilean education was not practical, and for Frei, not humanistic enough.[13] The most effective parts of the book are those in which the spirit of Frei's mentors, the fighting Jesuits, and the influence of Maritain are visible: his graphic descriptions of the physical suffering and moral degradation of the common people, and his remarks on the relations between the upper and the lower classes:

For the moment it is assumed that much can be achieved through private charity, "as if charity could cover up the violation of justice" (Quadragesimo anno). Some well-intentioned gentlemen attend the distribution of free milk,

[12] Francisco A. Encina, *Nuestra inferioridad económica: sus causas, sus consecuencias* (new ed.; Santiago de Chile: Editorial Universitaria, S. A., 1955), and Alberto Edwards Vives, *La fronda aristocrática* (Santiago de Chile: Editorial Del Pacífico, S. A., 1959).

[13] Thus Frei pleaded for the reintroduction of Latin, the study of which in secondary schools had been abolished by an anticlerical government in the nineteenth century, and for a university that would be a center of higher learning instead of a vocational school turning out lawyers, doctors, and architects.

visit orphanages, and sometimes even show up in the slums. But in general these visits engender more rancor than gratitude. . . . The people cannot be saved by the distribution of milk, or by visits from gentleman sociologists. They will be saved by an internal movement of renovation, by which they will acquire dignity and the means to build for themselves and by their own efforts a rational and profoundly human life. . . . The material conditions that the people lack are due to them in justice and not as a favor. When this has been achieved, the gulf can be closed. Not before. And all these pious or philanthropic institutions, however well-intentioned, will not help to solve our social problem or to bring the hostile classes one inch closer to each other. . . .[14]

Unknown Chile is the picture of a country whose social system combines the worst features of laissez-faire individualism and state socialism — a disjointed agglomeration of inefficient, inadequate, and unproductive institutions that have come into being on the basis of improvised and accidental decisions made without a guiding principle. In essence Frei arrived at the same conclusions as the CEPAL[15] economist Jorge Ahumada twenty years later in a far more thorough and documented study, *En vez de la miseria:* "The crisis is total, and it has its origin in the lack of harmony of the disjointed institutions, activities, and values of the nation."[16]

The remedies proposed by Frei were augmentation and diversification of industrial production, heavier taxation of the foreign-owned mines, and an agrarian reform accompanied by the development of coopera-

[14] Frei, *Chile desconocido, op. cit.,* p. 86.

[15] CEPAL (Comisión Económica para América Latina), the economic commission of the Organization of American states (OAS).

[16] Jorge Ahumada, *En vez de la miseria* (2nd ed.; Santiago de Chile: Editorial Del Pacífico, S. A., 1958), p. 17.

tives and the modernization of techniques. Tacked onto these strictly practical measures, in a rather unmotivated fashion, was a project for "an organization of the state in which economic forces have true influence"[17] — that is, the corporate state: "Corporative organization signifies the integration of economic power with political power."[18] It is significant, however, that Frei did not advocate the creation of national and regional corporations by state decree but declared that these bodies should be the result of a natural process.[19] Nor did he advocate the abolition of democracy and of the party system; if one party alone was not strong enough to form a government, then the reform measures should be introduced by a government coalition of all those forces willing to support such a program.[20]

Apart from his profession of faith in the corporate state, a chimerical economic ideal also highly fashionable in European Catholic circles in the 1930's, one finds little trace of fascist influence in Frei's book. There is patriotic concern for the welfare of the country but none of the chauvinistic arrogance and contempt for other nations that is the very essence of fascism. Indeed there is no hatred of any kind in the book, no appeal to the baser emotions. Instead *Unknown Chile* shows a preoccupation with the dignity of the common man that is the exact opposite of the fascists' disdain for the weak and glorification of brute strength.[21]

[17] Frei, *Chile desconocido, op. cit.,* p. 162.
[18] *Ibid.,* p. 164.
[19] *Ibid.,* p. 163.
[20] *Ibid.,* p. 143.
[21] This preoccupation with the dignity of the common man is also a characteristic of such movements as the MNR (Movimiento Nacionalista Revolucionario) in Bolivia and the Peronistas in Argentina, which came into being under strong fascist influence and in their early stages maintained close contact with Nazi Germany and Fascist

It is true that in *Unknown Chile* Frei also demonstrated a marked preference for a strong government working to achieve a preconceived plan. The list of governments that in his opinion came up to this specification is surprising. "Today," he wrote, "a government must have guiding ideas and a plan to carry out. Roosevelt, Hitler, Blum, Mussolini, Stalin, Salazar, Van Zeeland are clearly manifestations of a tendency noticeable in every political system." Thus to Frei German and Soviet totalitarianism, the milder Italian and Portuguese forms of fascism, and democratic regimes of three different tendencies all appeared to be on the same plane. It is as difficult for a Latin American to judge the political situation in Europe as for a European to understand that in Latin America, and for the same reason: Each is apt to use a yardstick that is perfectly valid on his own continent but does not apply to the other one.

The basic problem in most Latin American countries is that of a superannuated social structure, dating back to colonial days, that impedes economic progress and obliges a large sector of the population to live in subhuman conditions. Social change is necessary in Latin America if the common man is to attain dignity. It is by this yardstick that Eduardo Frei measured the governments of Hitler, Stalin, Mussolini, Salazar, Roosevelt, Blum, and Van Zeeland; and all of them — communist, fascist, and democratic regimes — appeared to him to be moving in the same direction and striving for the same goal: orderly, planned social change.

Yet the problem of Europe in the 1930's was very

Italy. This shows that fascism in Latin America was not quite the same phenomenon as in Europe and should not be judged as harshly.

different. It was not that of social change per se but of whether a frontal attack on the rights of the citizen and the dignity of man could be repulsed.

Furthermore European fascism had arisen as a reaction to the communist danger and therefore enjoyed the sympathies and financial backing of industrialists, financiers, and big landowners. In Latin America, on the other hand, communism was far too weak to threaten the positions of the financial, industrial, and agrarian oligarchy. The oligarchy was not driven to desperate measures of self-defense, and the fascist groups that sprang up in Latin America in imitation of European fascism therefore did not enjoy its backing. For this reason the link between fascism and the oligarchy in Europe escaped Frei's attention: There was no such link in his own country. Only in one country was the link perfectly obvious even to the Latin American observer: Spain, where the fascist Franco regime was fighting a war in order to restore the property and privileges of the oligarchy. It is significant that the Franco regime was not mentioned in Frei's book and that the first European fascist group with which the Chilean Falangists became thoroughly disillusioned was their Spanish namesake. When the Spanish Republic was defeated in 1939, the Chilean Falangists supported the campaign to admit the Republican refugees to their country.

THE FALANGE MOVES LEFT

A publisher's note to Frei's book stated

The Conservative Youth of Chile constitutes a phalanx with an advanced social program, which differentiates it from its stem, the Conservative Party, to whose rejuvenation and animation it contributes. Eduardo Frei is one of the prime movers in this task of transformation undertaken by the Conservative Youth of Chile, which in certain respects is drawing closer to the leftist movements.

We thus see that as early as 1937, only two years after its foundation, the leftward evolution of the Falange was under way.

This evolution was inevitable. The Falangists were deeply convinced of the necessity of radical social reform. In this they found their natural ally in the Left. On the other hand, the oligarchy that controlled their own Conservative Party did not want change and greatly resented the Falangists' efforts to "rejuvenate" and "animate" the party by pushing it leftward.

Matters came to a head on the occasion of the 1938 presidential election. The candidate of the Liberals and Conservatives was Gustavo Ross, a banker and President Arturo Alessandri's Minister of Finance. Ross was a firm believer in the blessings of uninhibited free enterprise and also in the need for a firm hand with the lower classes if they happened to balk at any sacrifice that might be demanded of them in the interests of the economy. He thus represented all that the Falangists abhorred, and in the inner councils of the Conservative Party they stubbornly opposed his nomination. They demanded that the presidential candidate be "a man who represents a sure guarantee of social peace, in order to ensure that the coming unavoidable social and political changes will be implemented in an atmosphere of social harmony," and insisted that the candidate should be someone "respectful of the human liberty of friends and enemies alike and of the lawful rights of all Chileans without any exception whatsoever."[22]

When Ross was actually nominated, the Falange refused to give him its official support and told its supporters that each should vote according to the demands of his conscience. In the election Ross was defeated by the Popular Front candidate Pedro Aguirre Cerda, a Radical, by the narrow margin of 4,000 votes. The Conservative Party thereupon decided to break the spirit of its unruly youth organization by purging its leadership. The Falange refused to submit to the purge and constituted itself as an independent political party.

From the first the new party's record was left of center — as well as impeccably democratic. Its parliamentary delegation supported the Popular Front government of President Aguirre Cerda (1938–1942) and in the 1942 presidential election joined the Socialists and Communists in supporting another Radical, Juan Antonio Ríos, against the candidate of the Right, ex-dictator Ibáñez. Later Eduardo Frei, by then the undisputed leader of the Falange, joined President Ríos' cabinet as Minister for Public Works. In 1947 and 1948 the Falange opposed President Gabriel Gonzáles Videla's measures against the Communist Party. In 1954 it participated in the leftists' protest demonstrations against the overthrow of the Arbenz government in Guatemala. During the administration of President Ibáñez (1952–1958) it was a member of the opposition bloc of Radicals, Liberals, Conservatives, and Communists. When the rightist government of President Jorge Alessandri took over in 1958, the Falange formed a parlia-

[22] Silva Bascuñán, *op. cit.,* p. 94.

mentary opposition bloc with the Socialists and Communists.

The Falange's frequent cooperation with the Communists does not mean that it was a party of fellow travelers or was under any illusions about the nature of communism. The Falangists' attitude toward communism is defined by one of its leaders, Jaime Castillo, in his book *El problema comunista:*

Our opinion is that of Alcide de Gasperi: As long as the Communist Party stays within the democratic norms, it should not be subject to repressive laws. . . .[23]

Legal toleration of the Communist Party does not signify suspension of the ideological struggle or a passive or indifferent attitude. . . .[24]

Its consistently pro-Russian character makes long-term collaboration with the Communist Party in a constructive policy impossible.[25]

The object of Soviet policy is the world triumph of the Soviet Union, and not the national problems of Chile. . . . Nevertheless all this does not mean that there cannot be short-term agreements in regard to specific practical policies. . . .[26]

DEMOCRACIA CRISTIANA

For the first nineteen years of its existence as an independent party the Falange's numerical strength remained negligible. It polled 3.4 per cent of the valid votes in the 1941 parliamentary elections, 2.6 per cent in 1945, 3.9 per cent in 1949, and 2.9 per cent in

[23] Jaime Castillo Velasco, *El problema comunista* (Santiago de Chile: Editorial Del Pacífico, S. A., 1955), p. 205.
[24] *Ibid.*, p. 206.
[25] *Ibid.*, p. 210.
[26] *Ibid.*, p. 214.

1953. In the municipal elections of 1956 its vote at long last showed an upward trend, and in the parliamentary elections of 1957 it jumped to 9.4 per cent.[27] In the same year the Falange fused with a small Christian Social group that had split off from the Conservative Party, and it changed its name to Christian Democratic Party. Encouraged by its 1957 election success, the Christian Democratic Party decided to put up a candidate of its own, Eduardo Frei, for the presidential election of 1958. Frei ran a poor third behind Jorge Alessandri, the victorious candidate of the Liberals and Conservatives, and Salvador Allende of the Socialist-Communist FRAP alliance. However, he did poll more than 20 per cent of the total vote, and his candidacy served both to make him known throughout the country and to consolidate the organization of his party and its position with the electorate. In the 1961 parliamentary elections the Christian Democratic vote rose further to 15.9 per cent, and in the municipal elections of 1963 to 22.8 per cent.[28]

In the period of this astonishing rise the percentage of votes won by the Socialists and Communists also rose, although not spectacularly; the Radicals maintained their percentage; and the vote of the Liberals and Conservatives increased numerically, although not enough to enable them to maintain their old percentage. A number of ephemeral parties that formed the caudillo Ibáñez' retinue in the early 1950's disappeared, but apparently most of their voters either returned to the traditional parties of the Center and Right or were

[27] These percentages are the official ones of the Electoral Register, as reproduced in Guilisasti, *op. cit.*, p. 208.
[28] *Ibid.*

absorbed by the Left. The rise of the Christian Democrats was thus brought about less by defections from other groups than by new votes, that is, by the votes of citizens who were either too young or too remote from political life to have voted in previous elections.

The standard explanation for the phenomenon of a new party that suddenly grows big and becomes a decisive factor in a country's political life is that the people are tired of the old parties and old formulas and are looking for something new. There is always much truth in this platitude, but it is far too vague to be satisfactory. To find the real explanation of the phenomenon one must ask: What people are looking for something new, what is this something for which they are looking, and why are they looking for it?

In Chile certain social groups in the cities are the people looking for something new. The Chilean Christian Democrats are an urban party. They have only just begun to take roots in the countryside and will not be firmly established there until a Christian Democratic government has implemented a real agrarian reform.

As a result of both the growth of industry in the last two decades and the extremely poor living conditions in the rural areas, Chilean cities are growing at a breathtaking pace. The main strength of the Christian Democrats lies precisely in the new strata of the urban population. The party is strong in the workers' settlements and *callampas*, or shantytowns, that house the multitude of those who have fled the countryside. And it is even stronger among the white-collar workers of the commercial and industrial enterprises that have come into being or have been greatly expanded in the course of the last two decades and among the many technicians and professionals who have come out of the universities in this period.

These vast new strata of the population demand a better life, but they do not reach for the moon: They want better food, a home, furniture, a radio, then perhaps a television set and a refrigerator, and, more than all this, better schools and more opportunities in life for their children.

To many of them the Marxist answer to these demands, namely, that all this can be achieved only through class war, revolution, and national liberation, is unsatisfactory. They reject this answer, first, because they doubt whether a campaign of revolution and national liberation would be victorious and, second, because around them and in their midst they see fairly frequent examples proving that even within the present unsatisfactory system perseverance, ability, and luck make it possible to achieve a higher living standard.

In the presidential election of 1964 more than half the voters in the shantytown and working-class districts of Santiago and Valparaíso preferred the Christian Democratic to the Marxist candidate. These hard figures show that the Marxist message had failed to come through to those whom it most directly concerns. The Marxist parties have not been able to take advantage of the vast social and economic changes of the last twenty years, which have turned Chile into a predominantly urban nation. In other words, these parties are not modern; their techniques and their answers to the everyday problems of mid-century Chile are not up to date. This is hardly surprising in view of the fact that their picture of the world is still basically that described in Lenin's *Imperialism,* a textbook written half a century ago, and that they have made little or no effort to bring this superannuated picture into line with present-day reality.

IDEOLOGY AND PROGRAM

The Chilean Christian Democrats' picture of the ideal society is as far removed from present-day Latin American reality as the Marxist dream of the communist society. What makes their concept more acceptable to the average citizen than that of the Marxists is that according to the Christian Democrats the ideal society of the future can be achieved by a gradual evolution of the social structure and within the framework of the democratic political system — and without a life-and-death national liberation struggle against the great power that dominates the Western Hemisphere.

The Christian Democrats believe that the world is moving toward a new social system that they call "communitarianism," which, according to Eduardo Frei,

is a social structure in which the community formed by those who work in the same industrial or agrarian enterprise is of basic importance. This implies the ending of the profound class conflict inherent in our present social organization, in which a fairly small group possesses the power, the resources, and the authority that go with control over property, whereas the vast majority are wage earners. The communitarian ideal thus demands an order of things in which capital and labor are no longer divorced and therefore do not come into conflict, no longer belong to different groups but are united in the same hands.[29]

The concept of communitarianism thus bears a

29 In *ibid.*, p. 214.

striking resemblance to the system of workers' self-management now being at least ostensibly implemented in Yugoslavia. The Yugoslav system, however, is a product of revolution, expropriation, and dictatorship. The Chilean Christian Democrats reject this road:

> The communitarian road does not pretend to impose its system from above, by decree, and from one day to the next, as a hard and rigid mechanism that, by the power of the state, is applied to the whole population, as has happened under the socialist regime of those countries ruled by communism. Such a procedure is not compatible with democracy. It presupposes a brutal dictatorship, which in practice is exercised even against the working class itself. . . .
>
> Communitarianism is not a machine or a yoke to which man must submit whether he likes it or not. It is a gradual process running in the same direction as the development of modern society.[30]

One may indeed claim that the industrially developed countries of the West are already moving in the direction of a communitarian society, that is, "an order of things in which capital and labor . . . no longer belong to different groups but are united in the same hands." A silent managerial revolution has greatly increased the powers of management at the expense of those of ownership. At the same time, ownership is becoming increasingly widespread and anonymous, while labor in some European countries, through its trade-union delegates, is already represented on the boards of directors of big enterprises. In the very long run this may well lead to a system resembling that of the Yugoslavs: with nominal control over the enterprise resting with

[30] *Ibid.*, p. 215.

the workers, while actual control is in the hands of a manager whose legal status is that of their employee.

The concept of communitarianism is extremely useful to the Christian Democratic party leaders because it enables them to justify essential points of their immediate program, which would otherwise appear to be purely pragmatic, as necessary steps toward the establishment of the communitarian system.

Thus the Christian Democrats intend to do away with the legal restrictions that at present prevent the Chilean trade unions from combining into powerful federations capable of nationwide collective bargaining. By this move the Christian Democrats hope to win the workers away from the Marxist Left and to build up a really powerful and effective trade-union movement under Christian Democratic control. A strong trade-union movement can of course also be justified as a precondition for the establishment of "workers' control" in a communitarian society.

The Christian Democratic agrarian reform plan envisages the expropriation of the big estates, which are to be operated as agricultural cooperatives under the supervision of managers appointed by the state. At a later stage, when sufficient financial means are available, the land is to be partitioned, but the cooperative structure is to be maintained. This aim, and the stress on the development of cooperatives in other fields of economic activity, can also be explained as a step toward a communitarian society in which "the free play of individual appetites" is replaced by the principle of cooperation.

The Christian Democratic reform program further envisages radical decentralization of the state administrative machine. This decentralization is deemed necessary in order to render administration more efficient and less costly and at the same time to stimulate local initiative. But decentralization, that is, local autonomy, is also an indispensable feature of a communitarian society based on the self-management of small units.

In the communitarian society of the future there will hardly be room for foreign industrial enterprises on Chilean soil. For the time being, however, the Christian Democrats realistically reject the nationalization of the big American-owned copper mines whose ore is a decisive factor in the Chilean balance of payments. What they do insist on is the "Chileanization" of the mines. This means not only the gradual replacement of North American by Chilean managing personnel but also, and more importantly, the coordination of the copper companies' policies with the interests of the Chilean state, which according to the Christian Democrats is still lacking at present. It would be in the interests of Chile if all the copper ore mined in Chilean mines were processed in the country, but the companies prefer to process at least part of it in their existing establishments abroad. And since the production costs of Chilean copper are low, it would be in the Chilean interest greatly to increase copper production, since this would bring increased revenue even if the world market price of copper declined. In fact, the Christian Democrats demand a twofold increase in Chilean copper production from the present annual level of about 600,000 tons to 1.2 million tons, which would solve the country's balance-of-payments problem for some years to come.

President Jorge Alessandri failed to obtain an increase in copper production or processing because the guarantees demanded by the companies were unacceptable to the Chilean parliament. The Christian Democrats believe that they can do better by forcing a showdown. They assume that the copper companies, faced with the threat of nationalization, would prefer to provide the investment funds needed to step up copper production and processing.

The Christian Democrats' copper policy is but one facet of their "assertive nationalism." In a highly revealing speech in 1954 Eduardo Frei contrasted this "assertive nationalism," which he defined as a policy of "honorable association" and "constructive cooperation," with the policies of *entreguismo*, or surrender, and violent nationalism, or "strategic hatred." He said

If the United States would understand that the better friends of inter-American cooperation are those who defend the legitimate interest of their peoples; if the United States understood that those who speak frankly today will be far more capable of conducting a policy of solidarity tomorrow, then that would constitute an effective step toward inter-American solidarity.

I believe that no conscientious Latin American can deny the fact that for this continent, for its economic development, its future prosperity, and the well-being of the agricultural, industrial, and mining workers, cooperation with the United States is fundamental. If this cooperation is lacking, the masses of these countries will undergo many years of grave suffering and backwardness. Those who use strategic hatred are, fundamentally, sacrificing the people. They are the counterpart of the *entreguistas*.

Those really working for true friendship between Latin America and the United States are those who demand a policy of justice, of frankness, of cooperation, a policy not based on weakness but on firmness in stating the facts. It is necessary to convince North American public opinion that in the same way as the workers of the United States reached a level of social equity by means of a hard struggle, and this without prejudice to the country's progress, Latin America also must achieve international equity and real economic cooperation by way of a hard struggle; by defending its resources, defending its workers, defending its life. . . .

I am profoundly disturbed when I am told that we must ask the United States for help in maintaining our democracy, as I am also disturbed when I hear that some people want to ask for its help in overthrowing some South American governments — even if these be dictatorships. Democracy will be won by the nations themselves, or it will not be won. For nations do not acquire dignity, freedom, and equality as a gift from outside but by winning them from within.[31]

The Chilean Christian Democrats may thus be defined as a nationalist (though not irrationally nationalistic) party with a program of practical reforms that are seen as steps toward the achievement of an ideal: communitarianism.

In itself, communitarianism is merely an interesting theory, a concept of what society may one day be like. It is not enough to inspire men to enthusiasm and sacrifice — especially since they are told that the trend of historical development runs in this direction in any case. But if one believes that the present-day capitalist system is evil, that it is not in accordance with the commands of God, then the concept of communitarianism is at once charged with emotional significance; it becomes a goal for which to strive.

Chilean Christian Democracy was founded by men who rejected contemporary Chilean and Latin Amer-

[31] Chilean Senate report on the Caracas OAS conference of April 1954, quoted from Eduardo Frei M., *Pensamiento y acción* (Santiago de Chile: Editorial Del Pacífico, S. A., 1956), pp. 227 ff.

ican reality and were determined to strive for a society more in keeping with the spirit of Christianity. These men have since been joined by many sober technicians who believe in the need for social change not for religious reasons but simply because they consider the present system wasteful and ineffective. But something of the old religiously inspired fervor is still to be found among the party cadres.

Faith and fervor give cohesion and dynamism to a movement, but they also inevitably inspire mistrust and antagonism. The stronger a faith or ideology, the stronger also the reaction. This is especially true of a Christian movement in a country like Chile.

According to an estimate given to us by the Sociological Institute of the University of Chile only about one third of Chile's population is under the influence of the Church. The other two thirds are indifferent, frequently anticlerical, and even include a sizable minority of militant atheists. The Christian Democrats therefore lay great stress on the fact that they are not a clerical party. Eduardo Frei himself has stated

> The Christian Democratic Party is not a denominational or clerical party, as some would assume. . . .
> Christian Democracy has never endeavored to implement a policy of Church privileges, let alone to impose religious belief or to establish Catholicism as the official state doctrine. . . . [There is] a vast Christian Democratic literature on this matter. This subject has been pondered and discussed by various authors, such as Maritain, Lebret, Mounier, Ducatillon, Athayde, and others.
> Nor is Christian Democracy a Catholic or denominational party demanding that its members be believers, or aspiring to assume the factual or formal representation of the Church or of Catholicism.

Quite to the contrary.

We have spent our life maintaining that no party has the right to proclaim itself the Catholic party, to assume the representation of the Church, or to take itself to be the only "orthodox" vessel for those Catholics who are active in public life.

We would thus hardly be likely not to fall into these same errors.

The name Christian Democracy may be misunderstood. It does not stand for an exclusive democracy, only for Christians, or even a democracy controlled by the Christians. . . .

For Christian Democracy, society itself approaches or deviates from Christian values in the measure in which it approaches or deviates from a human fellowship impregnated with love, which is the supreme law of Christianity. We are not concerned with creating a state that is "decoratively Christian," full of ostentation and religious emblems, like some that are at present in existence, but a state that is Christian in essence. . . .

Our political activity has always made it clear that the religious plane must be distinguished from the temporal plane. We have maintained that Catholics can hold different and even contrary opinions on temporal or political matters. It is absurd that in the political field there should be alignments such as that of Catholics against non-Catholics. We have done everything in our power to overcome these quarrels of the past, and we shall not be the ones who revive them.[32]

A REFORMIST PARTY

Fidel Castro has aptly called the Chilean Christian Democrats a reformist party, as opposed to the revolutionaries of the Marxist Left. In its program and policies it is indeed akin to the European social democrats and

[32] Guilisasti, *op. cit.*, pp. 218 ff.

not to the Christian Democratic parties of the Old World. Like the European social democrats, it has a pragmatic program of social and economic reforms that are justified as being necessary steps toward an ideal lying far in the future, an ideal to be attained not by a revolutionary act but by a gradual ripening of conditions.

The Chilean Christian Democrats have, however, one great advantage over the social democrats of Europe: They are not hampered by the historical tradition of nineteenth-century socialism. According to this tradition those who labor with their hands are the salt of the earth; they are the instrument by which history will bring about the liberation and salvation of mankind. The doctrine that the manual workers are the main force, and the white-collar workers and intellectuals only auxiliaries, in the struggle for a better future is strong even in such social democratic parties as the British Labour Party, which is not Marxist in origin and has many intellectuals among its leaders.

This doctrine naturally antagonizes the nonmanual workers. Especially since World War II the social democratic parties have struggled to break down the barrier thus artificially created, but not even the British Labour Party, which has made the most determined efforts, has been completely successful.

It is often asked why there are no large social democratic parties in Latin America. The reason is that workers' parties are the product of a specifically European historical tradition dating back to the nineteenth century.[33] This tradition is absent not only in Latin

---

[33] And perhaps even much farther back in history, to the guild

America but also in the entire Western Hemisphere. That is why so many attempts to form workers' parties have failed in this hemisphere. The usual pattern in Latin America is that of large populist parties of both blue-collar and white-collar workers, professionals, businessmen, and in some cases also peasants. The Venezuelan Acción Democrática and URD, the Peruvian APRA and Acción Popular, the Mexican PRI (Partido Revolucionario Institucional), and the Bolivian MNR are such parties. Chile, with its two proletarian Marxist parties, is apparently an exception, but now in that country a populist party, Christian Democracy, has also arisen and is successfully challenging the Marxists in their proletarian strongholds.

We thus see that Chilean Christian Democracy is a specifically Latin American phenomenon. It is a phenomenon of mid-twentieth-century urban Latin America, a Latin America of teeming cities whose problems are very different from those of both the great European cities and the old Latin America of latifundia and adobe villages.

---

system of the Middle Ages. The guild system was still in existence in Germany in the first half of the nineteenth century; the men who first spread the gospel of socialism and communism in Germany and laid the foundations of the socialist movement in that country — Wilhelm Weitling, many members of Marx' and Engels' League of Communists, and others — were mostly wandering guild craftsmen, and it is precisely German socialism with its strong tradition of proletarian isolationism and guild exclusiveness that became dominant in the Socialist International. The Latin American working class, formed only in the second half of the nineteenth century and the first half of the twentieth century, lacks the guild tradition of exclusivity.

6

 THE PRESIDENTIAL ELECTION OF 1964

It is most unusual for an election in one of the smaller Latin American countries to be of vital importance for the entire continent and of relevance to the international balance of power as was the Chilean presidential election of September 4, 1964.

One of the two main candidates in this election, Salvador Allende, was the representative of a coalition of the pro-Soviet Communists and the Socialist Party, which in Chile is the party of extreme Latin American nationalism. His election would have meant that in fact though perhaps not in form Chile would have left the inter-American alliance. It would have given new impetus to the Latin American extreme Left, which had entered a period of decline after the Caribbean crisis of 1962, and might well have encouraged the Soviet Union to resume its Cold War offensive in Latin America, which had come to a halt as a result of that crisis.

THE CANDIDATES

The government of President Jorge Alessandri (1958–1964) depended on the parliamentary support of a coalition of Conservatives, Liberals, and Radicals that called itself the Democratic Front (Frente Democrático). The parliamentary opposition, which usually voted in a compact bloc, was composed of the Christian Democrats, the Socialists, the Communists, and PADENA. The three last-named parties were linked together in a formal alliance, the Popular Action Front (FRAP).

Early in 1963 the leftist FRAP coalition nominated the Socialist Senator Salvador Allende as their candidate for the 1964 presidential election.[1] The Frente Democrático followed suit with the nomination of the Radical Senator Julio Durán, while the Christian Democrats nominated their leader, Senator Eduardo Frei. Jorge Prat, a collaborator of the late President Ibáñez, was nominated as an independent candidate by rightist nationalist circles.

In the 1963 municipal elections the parties of the Frente Democrático had polled 46 per cent of the valid vote, as against 31.2 per cent for FRAP and 22.8 per cent for the Christian Democrats. Jorge Prat was assumed to command a block of little more than 5 per cent of the vote. The candidate of the Frente Democrático, Julio Durán, was therefore expected to win by a comfortable margin.

Durán, however, was heavily handicapped by the fact that he was not well known outside his own party and was a machine politician — a profession not held

[1] See Chapter 3.

in high esteem in Chile. Warning voices were thus raised in the government camp, pointing out that personality to the Chilean voter counted more than party affiliation, and that in a three- or four-cornered contest Durán would be in serious trouble.

These warnings were fully justified by the result of a parliamentary by-election in the agricultural province of Curicó in March 1964. In the municipal elections of 1963 the province of Curicó had given 48 per cent of its vote to the parties of the government coalition. Then, only a year later, the Frente Democrático vote slumped to 32 per cent, the FRAP vote rose from 31 per cent to 41 per cent, and that of the Christian Democrats from 21 per cent to 27 per cent.

Durán had campaigned for the local candidate of the Frente Democrático and had declared that he would consider the by-election result a valid test of his prospects in the coming presidential election. True to his word he announced the withdrawal of his candidature, thus relieving his Liberal and Conservative allies from their obligations. The Frente Democrático then broke up. The Liberals and Conservatives declared their unconditional support of the Christian Democrat Eduardo Frei, thereby demonstrating the pliancy and ability to face up to unpleasant decisions that is said to be characteristic of the Chilean oligarchy.

The Radicals subsequently persuaded Durán to stay in the presidential contest as the candidate of their party alone. Although they fully realized that he no longer stood the slightest chance, they considered this action necessary in order to maintain the unity of the party. A decision to support either Frei or Allende would certainly have caused the party to break up into its two opposing wings. Furthermore there was the possibility that in the election neither Frei nor Allende would win an absolute majority. In that case parliament would have to decide between them, and there the strong Radical representation would be in an excellent bargaining position.

Since the independent candidate Jorge Prat had also announced his withdrawal, the election took on the aspect of a straight contest between a Marxist extremist, Salvador Allende, and a moderate leftist, Eduardo Frei, with the former favorite Julio Durán reduced to the role of a mere onlooker. Besides the support of the two Marxist parties and of the non-Marxist PADENA, Allende had that of some defectors from the Radical Party and even of an aristocratic Liberal senator.[2] Frei was supported by the Christian Democrats, the Liberals, the Conservatives, and by defectors from PADENA and from the Socialists.[3]

[2] The Liberal was Senator Gregorio Amunátegui, one of the most prominent figures of his party. The Senator explained his defection to Allende by the long-standing anticlerical tradition of his family. The Radicals were a group of leftist doctrinaires led by Alejandro Ríos Valdivia and Senator Exequiel González Madariaga. They formed a group called the Movimiento Radical de Recuperación Doctrinaria, not to be confused with the vestigial Partido Radical Doctrinario founded by Arturo Olavarría in the late 1940's, which was also a member of the FRAP coalition. Other fellow-traveling members of FRAP were a Catholic group called "Movimiento Católico Allendista," led by the independent (now Socialist) Senator Rafael Tarud; an organization of reserve officers, the Frente Cívico-Militar, which donated an airplane for the use of campaign headquarters; and Senator Baltazar Castro's Vanguardia Popular, which left FRAP after the election.

[3] The Socialist defectors to Frei were of some importance. Their leader, Waldo Grez, was a prominent trade-union organizer who in 1960 had backed the Castroite trade-union chief Clotario Blest in his rebellion against the Communist and Socialist party bosses. The main motive for his defection appears to have been a personal

The Christian Democrat Eduardo Frei, a fifty-three-year-old lawyer, had been the undisputed leader of his party for two decades and its representative in the Senate for sixteen years. He was widely respected for his integrity. His consistency of purpose, which his opponents frequently interpreted as mere rigidity, is illustrated by the fact that in his first book, written in 1937,[4] his practical proposals for the economic and social transformation of his country were basically the same ones that today constitute his party's reform program. He was not a brilliant orator. An intellectual of courteous and even-tempered personality, he had little in common with the classic image of the Latin American caudillo; yet he somehow had the caudillo's gift of inspiring devotion and enthusiasm.

Frei's opponent, the fifty-six-year-old Socialist Salvador Allende, was a doctor of medicine who had turned to politics as his career. He became a member of the Chamber of Deputies as early as 1937, at the age of twenty-nine, and from 1939 to 1942 served as Minister of Health in President Pedro Aguirre Cerda's cabinet. Later, as one of the Socialist Party's most prominent personalities, he was deeply involved in that party's bitter quarrel with the Communists. But in 1952, when the Socialists decided to support the presidential candidature of the former dictator Carlos Ibáñez, Allende left the party and defiantly announced his own candidature. He was supported by a Socialist splinter group and by the Communist Party, which at

feud with the autocratic Secretary-General of the Socialist Party, Raúl Ampuero.

[4] *Chile desconocido* (Santiago de Chile: Ediciones Ercilla, 1937). See Chapter 5.

that time had no legal status[5] and was looking for an ally with whose help it could work its way back to political respectability. Allende's candidature had no hope of success, and he actually polled only 50,000 votes, coming in last in a field of four. Yet his entire future career came to be based on what at the time had appeared to be a brave but entirely futile gesture of defiance against the wave of Ibañista sentiment that was sweeping the country. As it happened, President Ibáñez failed to fulfill the high expectations of his followers, while Allende gained stature as one of the leading figures of the parliamentary opposition against the autocratic president. In 1956 the main body of the Socialists, who had become thoroughly disillusioned with the president they had helped to elect, joined forces with Allende's Socialist splinter group and the Communists in the FRAP alliance. In 1957 the split in the Socialist Party was healed, and in the following year Allende, being the only Socialist leader wholly acceptable to the Communists, was FRAP's obvious choice as candidate for the presidency. He was again given little chance but did surprisingly well, polling 28.6 per cent of the total vote and coming in second in a field of five, only some 30,000 votes behind the victorious candidate of the two right-of-center parties, Jorge Alessandri.[6]

[5] The Communist Party had been suppressed in 1947 by President Gabriel González Videla, but police measures against it had been relaxed as early as 1949, and from then on its activities were tolerated, although it was not permitted to participate in the elections. It recovered its full legality at the end of President Ibáñez' term of office in 1958. See Chapter 3, pp. 53 ff.

[6] The 1958 presidential election results were: Jorge Alessandri (independent, supported by Liberals and Conservatives) — 389,900; Salvador Allende (FRAP) — 356,500; Eduardo Frei (Christian

His near-success in 1958 made it inevitable that he should again be nominated for the 1964 election. His two previous campaigns had made his name known even in the most far-removed parts of the country as a symbol for the social change that so many Chileans desired. He was generally assumed to be the effective leader of the united Left and thus a man who wielded real political power. Only the leading cadres of the FRAP parties, a few hundred people in all, realized that this was not the case. Actually Allende not only had no influence whatsoever on the policies of the allied Communist and PADENA parties but he was not even the leader of his own Socialist Party. That party was completely dominated by its autocratic Secretary-General, Raúl Ampuero, who was in total command of the party machine. In three decades of intensive political activity Allende had not been able to build up a machine of his own, or even the smallest group of personal friends, collaborators, and disciples. Nor did he have the faculty of captivating the masses. His platform manner was unimpressive, his speeches were delivered in a uniform key of querulous lamentation, and, although he is by no means unintelligent, it would be difficult to find either in his speeches or in his infrequent written pronouncements a single original thought or memorable turn of phrase. His greatest political asset was undoubtedly his remarkable skill in not arousing lasting enmity in anyone. Whatever he might have been at the time of his brave stand against Ibáñez, by 1964 he was the mere semblance of a leader, a man who was maintained in his position because

Democrat) — 255,700; Luis Bossay (Radical) — 192,100; Antonio Zamorano (independent) — 41,300.

those who held the real levers of command in the component parties of the FRAP alliance found him easy to manipulate and not dangerous to their interests.

In the 1964 presidential election campaign Allende acted as what might be termed a synthetic candidate, a figurehead going through all the motions of campaigning with a great show of energy, but not a strong personality providing effective leadership. Lacking leadership, the FRAP propagandists allowed themselves to be pushed completely into the defensive, and this position proved fatal for their campaign.

THE CAMPAIGN

The campaign platforms of the two principal candidates were made up of vast programs of social and economic reform, the details of which were worked out by teams of experts. The Christian Democrats proposed a "new deal" with the North American copper companies, obliging them to double copper production, provide installations for the processing of all the copper ore mined in Chile, and admit Chilean government participation in their policy decisions; an agrarian reform that would create 100,000 new peasant homesteads within six years; a stepping up of the government housing program; and a host of other things including an educational reform, a reform of the wage scale, an expansion of social services, increased scope for the trade unions, and administrative decentralization. The basic FRAP program envisaged an agrarian reform comprising the confiscation of the 2,000–3,000 large estates, which were to be divided into peasant farms, collectives, and state farms; the nationalization of the foreign-owned enterprises and the domestic monopolies; the centralization of credit and of foreign trade in the hands of the state; central planning of all productive activities; amplification of the housing program and social services; and other reforms also postulated by the Christian Democrats.

The FRAP program also envisaged an "independent," that is, neutralist foreign policy; the Christian Democrats did not propose to leave the inter-American alliance. Apart from this, the essential difference between the two programs was undoubtedly that the Christian Democrats emphasized the reform of existing institutions, while the main stress of the FRAP program was on nationalization and centralized state planning.

The FRAP program was clearly inspired by the Cuban example. Its main outline had been published as early as January 1963,[7] at a time when the impact of the Cuban revolution on Latin America in general and on Chile in particular was still so great that the measures implemented by Fidel Castro in the first stage of his revolution, in 1959 and the first half of 1960, appeared as the very minimum that a leftist election platform should demand. It was also clear that, since the implementation of this platform would inevitably lead to a conflict with the United States and would thereby place Chile in need of Soviet economic, political, and perhaps even military support, the FRAP government would not be able to maintain a neutralist position even if it should honestly desire to do so.

When the outline of the FRAP program was first published in January 1963, the Soviet Union had already suffered its great defeat in the Caribbean, but

[7] See *El Siglo*, January 25, 1963.

the full significance of the withdrawal of the Soviet missiles from Cuba was not yet apparent. It was not clear that at least for the time being the Soviet offensive in Latin America had ground to a halt, that the Caribbean crisis would paradoxically result in a lessening of tension between the Soviet Union and the United States, and that it also spelled defeat for the Cuban attempt to revolutionize Latin America under the protection of Soviet rocketry.

From that moment onward Cuba's glamor almost imperceptibly began to fade. The press reports of economic failure and political oppression found more and more credence with the Chilean public,[8] and by 1964 Cuba no longer served as a shining example but had actually become a source of embarrassment for the FRAP propagandists.

[8] Chile maintained diplomatic relations with Cuba until August 1964, and no official measures were taken to discourage visits to this center of revolutionary activity. Although nearly all Chilean visitors to Cuba were fervent admirers of the regime, the verbal reports they brought home often appeared to have been considerably less favorable than their published statements in the leftist press. By 1964 the impression that all was not going well in Cuba was widespread even in leftist extremist circles. The Chilean leftists' picture of conditions in Cuba tends to be far more realistic and better informed than their notions about the faraway Soviet Union, which is still idealized in exactly the same manner as it was by the European fellow travelers of the 1930's.

Two disappointed Chilean admirers of the Cuban revolution have published books dealing with their disillusionment. Matilde Ladrón de Guevara's *Adiós al Cañaveral: diario de una mujer en Cuba* (2nd ed.; Buenos Aires: Editorial Goyanarte, 1962) gives an impressionistic view of the disorganization and the rapid decline in the economic situation that prevailed in Cuba in the months following Castro's great triumph in the Bay of Pigs. In 1964 the Chilean airman Jacques Lagas, who had piloted a Cuban B-26 in the battle of the Bay of Pigs, published his *Memorias de un capitán rebelde* (Santiago de Chile: Editorial Del Pacífico, S. A., 1964), the intensely bitter book of an unsophisticated soldier trapped in a complicated web of political intrigue.

The FRAP election platform drawn up early in 1963 thus presupposed a psychological climate and an international situation that no longer prevailed in 1964. But while the FRAP leaders did not have the courage to swim against the stream, they also could not make up their minds to modify the platform in accordance with the change in conditions. Instead they took to the childish subterfuge of simply denying its ideological origin and refusing to discuss its foreign policy implications. Their program, they claimed, was a purely Chilean matter of practical social reforms, without any relevance to socialism, communism, Cuba, the Soviet Union, the world communist movement, or the Cold War, and it was impermissible to drag those extraneous subjects into the debate.[9] Their opponents naturally refused to limit the debate to those subjects that suited FRAP, and the country was deluged with posters,

[9] Allende in a typical statement:

This is no longer simple propaganda. It is psychological pressure, rape of the mind. This effort is aimed at pushing aside the national problems. They are trying to make the Chileans believe that in September they are not going to vote on the nationalization of the big mines and other foreign enterprises, the end of the big estates and the monopolies, the defeat of the oligarchy, the problems of housing, education, . . . etc. but on the Berlin Wall, Cuba, and Stalin. . . . They are trying to make us responsible for the actions of Fidel Castro's relatives, for what is happening between China and India, for the Hungarian counterrevolution. Anything to prevent the people from getting to know us. . . . (Quoted from the Communist review *Aurora*, Second Period, Year 1, No. 2 [April–June 1964], p. 7.)

The same Allende in a TV interview:

I do not listen much to the radio because I do not care to be asphyxiated by the propaganda against me and against the people's movement that is being made there hour for hour and minute for minute. I have strong nerves, I have power of resistance, but there is a limit. . . . (Quoted from *Arauco*, No. 55, August 1964, Special Number, "Allende en Televisión.")

pamphlets, newspaper articles, and radio programs warning the Chilean people that an Allende victory would mean the end of democracy, the installation of a dictatorship on the Cuban model, and the reduction of Chile to the status of a Soviet satellite.[10]

By what can have been only a deliberate decision of their campaign headquarters, the FRAP propagandists did not respond to this "campaign of fear," as they termed it, by rising to the defense of Cuba and the Soviet Union[11] but by long-winded complaints about their opponents' unfairness in daring to accuse the Chilean Socialists and Communists of not being good and law-abiding democrats. Allende himself became literally obsessed by this theme, and in the last months of the campaign he made it the central subject of his speeches; even his final querulous radio appeals were largely devoted to complaints instead of to the elucidation of his program.[12]

The FRAP alliance also tried to give itself an innocuous appearance by temporarily toning down the volume of its anti-American propaganda and by giving prominence to its non-Marxist fellow travelers. This strategy was based on the double assumption that FRAP already had the solid backing of the Chilean

[10] Eduardo Frei himself and his Christian Democratic aides did not join in this campaign. They concentrated on stressing the need for change and explaining their party's reform program, and they rarely even bothered to polemicize with their opponent.

[11] When the Alessandri government broke off relations with Cuba a few weeks before the election, the FRAP reaction was confined to a brief statement of protest by Allende, three Senate speeches, and a small meeting in a motion picture theater. The general strike that the Socialist Party's president of the trade unions had earlier threatened to call in the event of a rupture in relations did not materialize.

[12] See *El Mercurio*, September 3 and 4, 1964.

working class and that it would be able to capture a sizable proportion of the middle-class vote without making any programmatic concessions, by merely assuming outwardly moderate garb. On election day both assumptions turned out to be false.

THE ELECTION

On election day, September 4, 1964, 2,548,000 voters, or 87.41 per cent of the registered electorate, turned out to vote.[13] The election results were

Frei	1,418,000	(55.6%)
Allende	982,000	(38.5%)
Durán	125,000	(4.9%)[14]

As mentioned in Chapter 2 the male and female votes are counted separately. Frei obtained the majority of both the male and the female vote, but a much larger

[13] The population of Chile is approximately 8 million. The low percentage of registered voters is primarily due to the high birth rate, that is, to the high percentage of minors, but also to the fact that illiterates do not have the right to vote in Chile. The 1960 census showed an illiteracy rate of 16.4 per cent, as against 19.6 per cent in 1952. It may be assumed that the percentage of illiterates has further declined since 1960. Moreover, election propagandists frequently teach illiterates to sign their name, which is the only literacy test required for entry in the voters' register. It may thus be assumed that the percentage of illiterates excluded from the voting process was considerably lower than 16 per cent. Both registering and voting are compulsory in Chile, and unexplained absence of a registered voter from the polls is punishable by a prison sentence; hence the relatively low percentage of abstentions. Our election figures are based on the official results published by the Dirección del Registro Electoral and the Ministerio del Interior.

[14] The Radical candidate Julio Durán conducted a brisk campaign in which he demonstrated a rather appealing bluntness of speech and an attractive television manner. Nevertheless, the majority of Radical voters (more than 400,000 in the municipal elections of 1963) defected to either Allende or Frei.

one among the women, 63.3 per cent of whom voted for him as against 31.9 per cent for Allende. Of the male voters 49 per cent chose Frei and 45 per cent Allende.

The voting coincided to a marked degree with the figures of an opinion poll conducted by the Sociological Institute of the University of Chile,[15] which had been dismissed by political observers as giving an impossibly wide margin of victory to Frei. Even the Frei campaign headquarters had not ventured to predict so sweeping a victory, whereas the Allende headquarters had publicly predicted an advantage of around 200,000 votes for their candidate.[16]

In the presidential election of 1958 the FRAP candidate had polled 28.5 per cent of the total vote, and in the municipal elections of 1963 the combined strength of the FRAP parties had amounted to 31.5 per cent. In the light of these figures the FRAP performance in the 1964 election would appear to be highly creditable. Nevertheless a breakdown of the election results shows that the FRAP leaders had small cause for satisfaction: FRAP had failed in precisely those areas where it should have been strongest.

Frei had prevailed over Allende by an overwhelming margin in the cities and by a substantial margin both in the large towns and in the small towns and rural areas.[17] Of the total 1,159,400 votes in Chile's four

[15] Directed by Professor Eduardo Hamuy.

[16] See the Communist weekly newspaper *Vistazo*, No. 624, August 31, 1964.

[17] For our purposes we have considered as "cities" all those urban agglomerations that had more than 100,000 inhabitants according to the 1960 census, and as "large towns" all those that counted between 50,000 and 100,000 inhabitants. Such categories are of course inevitably somewhat arbitrary.

cities (Greater Santiago,[18] Valparaíso, Concepción, and Viña del Mar) the vote of the candidates had been

Frei	701,000 (60.7%)
Allende	403,500 (34.8%)

Frei had also prevailed in each of the country's six large towns (Antofagasta, Talca, Talcahuano, Chillán, Temuco, and Valdivia). Of their total of 183,200 votes

Frei	96,800 (52.8%)
Allende	75,800 (41.4%)

And Frei had also won in the small towns and rural areas, which had a total vote of 1,205,400

Frei	620,300 (51.4%)
Allende	502,800 (41.7%)

The four cities, which accounted for 45.5 per cent of the total vote, provided Frei with 49.7 per cent of his own total. Allende, on the other hand, received slightly more than half (51.2 per cent) of his vote from the small towns and rural areas, which accounted for 47.34 per cent of the total vote. In the entire country he clearly predominated in only one small region, the coal basin of Arauco. It consists of the department of Coronel (province of Concepción) and the neighboring province of Arauco, a depressed area of superannuated mines, with a high rate of unemployment and an extremely

[18] In accordance with the Corporación de Fomento de la Producción, *Geografía económica de Chile* (Santiago de Chile, 1962), we have considered "Greater Santiago" to comprise the following communes: Santiago, Conchalí, Providencia, Ñuñoa, Maipú, Quinta Normal, Renca, Quilicura, Lampa, Barrancas, Las Condes, La Florida, San Miguel, La Cisterna, La Granja, Puente Alto, Calera de Tango, and San Bernardo.

low wage level. In this traditionally Communist region the vote was:

Department of Coronel		Department of Arauco	
Allende	23,100	Allende	12,200
Frei	9,400	Frei	5,800

Allende also won the traditionally Socialist southernmost province of Magallanes, a wealthy sheep-raising region with the free port of Punta Arenas, but his margin was unexpectedly narrow (Allende 15,900 and Frei 13,400), and the three northernmost provinces of Tarapaca, Antofagasta, and Atacama, a desert region that is Chile's main copper and nitrate mining area. But here again Allende's margin was unexpectedly narrow (Allende 82,900 and Frei 79,800, a margin of 3,100 votes, whereas the official FRAP election expert had predicted a margin of 52,000 votes in Allende's favor).[19] In this region a majority of the ill-paid workers of the small Chilean copper mines, which are worked by primitive, almost medieval methods, voted for Allende, but he did not carry the commune of Calama, the seat of Anaconda's huge opencast copper mine Chuquicamata (Calama: Frei, 10,600 and Allende, 9,300). The workers of this American-owned mine, whose monthly wage averages U.S. $180 as against less than U.S. $30 in the small Chilean-owned mines, apparently did not take kindly to Allende's nationalization slogan.

In the larger urban areas Allende did not have a majority even among the subproletariat of the shantytowns. In the Departamento Pedro Aguirre Cerda (communes of San Miguel, La Cisterna, and La Granja), the

[19] See *Vistazo*, No. 624, August 31, 1964.

most extensive workers' settlement and shantytown area in Greater Santiago, Frei polled 91,200 against Allende's 76,600 votes. In the impoverished port of Valparaíso with its vast hillside slums, Frei won 75,100 against Allende's 42,500 votes. And even in the commune of Talcahuano (province of Concepción) with its steel mill and naval yard — an industrial area the squalor of which has to be seen to be believed — Frei prevailed with 14,100 against Allende's 13,600 votes.

Thus the appeal of the Marxist parties was strongest in provincial regions, among the workers of superannuated nineteenth-century coal mines and medieval copper mines. It was also strong, though not predominant, among the agricultural workers of the latifundia, the remnants of Spanish feudalism. But it failed to convince a majority of the proletariat in the modern urban Chile.

The FRAP leaders attributed their defeat to the "campaign of fear," the propaganda war waged against them with vastly superior means. It is indeed true that the financial resources of Frei's campaign headquarters were greatly superior to those of Allende. However, this superiority was certainly not effective in such working-class centers as San Miguel in Greater Santiago, the hillside slums of Valparaíso, or the industrial port of Talcahuano. These were the areas where the bulk of the Communist and Socialist party agitators were concentrated, and where they had every opportunity to counteract Christian Democratic propaganda. What is more, the inhabitants of these districts had been exposed to the full blast of Communist and Socialist party propaganda for years, and not only in the feverish last months of the election campaign.

The election results showed that neither the Communist nor the Chilean Socialist brand of Marxism-Leninism was of sufficient appeal to win a majority of the urban working-class votes. This weakness might have been remedied if the FRAP candidate's personality and campaign strategy had been of a nature to inspire confidence in the working-class electorate. As we have seen, that was not the case. One does not win confidence by tearful complaints about an opponent's unfairness or by trying to avoid any discussion of what up to a year ago had been one's most important propaganda asset.

To their own cadres the FRAP leadership had talked a very different language. The Socialist and Communist cadres had been brought to believe that September 4, 1964 would indeed not be an ordinary election day but the dawn of a new era, the birth of a second revolutionary socialist regime in the Western Hemisphere. Incessant assurances that victory was already theirs had kept them in a state of euphoria, and nothing had been done to prepare them for the eventuality of failure. The election defeat thus plunged them into black despair.

THE ELECTION AFTERMATH

Immediately after the election, the pro-Chinese elements in the Chilean Left resumed their factional activities. On October 4 Spartacus again held a Chinese revolution anniversary celebration in the Baquedano cinema, and the list of sponsors showed that the group had broken out of isolation and was now within reach of its objective — a broad pro-Chinese movement comprising elements of the independent Left, the Socialists, and even the left wing of the non-Marxist Radicals. The list included several of the most prominent independent figures of the FRAP coalition, leaders of PADENA, and two Radical senators.[20] The two main speakers were Socialist Deputy Clodomiro Almeyda and the independent Radical Deputy Ana Eugenia Ugalde. Two of the five senators sponsoring the meeting were Socialists: Salvador Allende, the defeated presidential candidate, and his campaign aide, Salomón Corbalán, a man generally considered to be one of Secretary-General Raúl Ampuero's most dependable followers.

This Chinese revolution anniversary meeting showed that the Communists' allies were no longer willing to pay any attention to Communist susceptibilities and that from now on the Communist Party would probably be able to maintain the FRAP alliance only at the price of constant humiliation. At the same time, Spartacus and other ultraleftist groups could expect to recruit a certain number of followers from among Communists who interpreted the election defeat as a vindication for the Chinese — and Cuban — doctrine of Violent Revolution.

But for the Communist Party leadership even this worry was not the major one. They knew very well that in the specific conditions prevailing in Chile, violent revolution was not feasible and probably would not be feasible in the future. A very determined effort to come to power by peaceful means had failed on September 4. The real issue for the party was whether it would have been better to avoid this defeat by sup-

[20] Hermes Ahumada and Jonás Gómez, both from the doctrinaire leftist sector of the Radical Party, which is known as the "Guatemalteco" group.

porting the Christian Democrats and then presenting their victory as a triumph for the forces of progress instead of reaching for power in coalition with the Socialists. It was the old issue that had been debated between the Communists and the Chilean Socialists for nearly thirty years: whether to have a broad alliance with limited aims or a narrow alliance with the aim of the total conquest of power.

In the 1930's the Socialists had reluctantly agreed to the Communist Popular Front formula of a broad alliance with limited aims. Twenty years later the Socialists had maneuvered the Communist Party into the Popular Action Front (FRAP), which was constructed according to their own formula of a "narrow" alliance of the two Marxist parties with only unimportant non-Marxist appendages.[21] This formula had now proved incapable

---

[21] In his speech to the February 1964 Socialist party congress, Secretary-General Raúl Ampuero made the following remarks on the conflict of opinion between Socialists and Communists on this issue:

> With time, two concepts gained profile within the people's movement. The Communist Party, in more or less mechanical reiteration of the 1938 picture, persisted in sustaining the need for a broad Democratic Front or National Liberation Front that would reach from the extreme Left with the workers' parties to the Center with the Radicals and Christian Democrats, at times not even excluding the possible participation of certain sectors of the Liberal Party. . . .
> We Socialists, on the other hand, had vivid memories of the experiences we had lived through at the time of the Popular Front. Ever more firmly we began to affirm a new concept, which denied to the Chilean bourgeoisie, as a class, all effective possibility of leading the anti-imperialist and antifeudal struggle or even to participate in it with loyalty and consistency. . . .
> Which, then, were the classes called upon to carry through the struggle against the old order? What was the nature of the revolutionary process that would enable us to unleash new, powerful forces for progress? The answers evolved only slowly but finally imposed themselves: Only the workers, the exploited, the uncompromised social strata were in a condition to deliver the historical battle against a superannuated and disintegrating

of rallying a majority of the Chilean working class. After defeat the Chilean Communists found themselves in opposition to a left-of-center progressive government — a position out of keeping with the party's traditions, with the inclinations of its leaders, and with its interests. By opposing a government that implemented reforms beneficial to the working class the Communists risked estranging their own working-class followers and driving them into the Christian Democratic camp.

The Socialist leader Ampuero's first reaction to the election defeat was a violent statement[22] proclaiming the need for implacable opposition to the Christian Democratic government and for continued unity of the FRAP coalition. In the same statement he maintained that the Sino-Soviet conflict had discredited the communist world movement and plunged it into mortal crisis, while he vindicated the independent line of the Chilean Socialists and their policy of avoiding foreign entanglements. From this he concluded that in the future only the Socialists would be capable of providing firm leadership for the united Left.

---

system; only a popular and democratic revolution of a clearly socialist tendency could construct a social system of a new type. Thus the barrier between the bourgeois-democratic and the socialist revolution, which had hitherto been impossible to surmount, would disappear, and both would be integrated in a unified and continuous process that would begin by removing the great obstacles to development — dependence on imperialism and the semifeudal system of land tenure — in order to crown their achievement by the establishment of ever-more advanced socialist relationships.

Thus the line of the Workers' Front was born.

Ampuero thus plainly and correctly stated that the formation of FRAP, or the "Workers' Front" as he termed it, spelled the victory of the Socialist formula of the "narrow front" over the Communist broad Popular Front formula.

22 See *Arauco*, No. 56, September 1964.

But this was an empty show of bravado. Actually the Socialists had been even harder hit by the election defeat than the Communists. It was the Socialist formula of a narrow "workers' alliance" that had been proved wrong by the election result. Also, the Communists had at least maintained their strength in their traditional strongholds, the mining districts, and these were the regions in which Allende had fared best. On the other hand, his election figures in such traditional Socialist strongholds as the copper mine of Chuquicamata, the port of Valparaíso, the Santiago workers' district of San Miguel, and the railroad workers' center of San Bernardo had been very disappointing. This showed that the Socialists were in even greater danger of Christian Democratic encroachment on their territory than the Communists.

The Chilean Socialists had always reproached their Argentinian comrades with narrow democratic prejudice in fighting against the Perón dictatorship instead of acknowledging it as a progressive force. It is indeed true that the workers had not been able to understand the Argentinian Socialists Party's negative attitude toward Perón and that in consequence that party had lost all influence on the Argentinian working class. The Chilean Socialists may now well suffer a very similar fate if their narrow antidemocratic prejudice pushes them into blind, unreasonable opposition against the new Christian Democratic government.

In the congressional elections of March 1965, Communist and Socialist expectations were again disappointed. Their strategists had taken it for granted that the bulk of those who had voted for Allende in the presidential election would remain in their camp.

Instead, their own vote dropped back to the level of the 1963 municipal elections, and their allies of the PADENA were almost completely annihilated. The Christian Democrats, on the other hand, won an absolute majority of the seats in the Chamber of Deputies.

In this atmosphere it appeared likely that both the crisis in the relations between the Communists and Socialists and the ideological crisis that had been brewing within each of them would soon become acute.

7

CONCLUSIONS

Chile is unique among Latin American countries in having a strong leftist movement that in its political tradition, its working-class origin and composition, its Marxist ideology, and its division into a Socialist and a Communist party appears to follow a European rather than a Latin American pattern. But appearances are deceptive. On closer inspection the Socialist Party of Chile loses all resemblance to the social democratic parties of Europe and reveals itself as a typically Latin American phenomenon: It is a party of militant nationalism with a record of participation in conspiracies and coups; its policies have always been determined by a leadership of middle-class intellectuals even though the party membership is largely of working-class stock. The Chilean Communists, on the other hand, lack a revolutionary tradition, and in spite of their totalitarian mentality and forms of organization, they have a history of collaboration with non-Marxist democratic groups.

The Cuban revolution has profoundly affected the policies of the Chilean Left.

When Fidel Castro assumed power in Cuba in January 1959, the Chilean Communists had only recently worked their way back to full legal status after an eleven-year period of clandestinity and semiclandestinity. They had achieved this, and acquired a measure of political respectability, by several years of patient collaboration with the democratic parties in opposing the autocratic tendencies of President Ibáñez. Simultaneously they had combined with the Socialists to form the Popular Action Front (FRAP); the FRAP candidate Salvador Allende had done surprisingly well in the 1958 presidential election. Yet even though Allende's near-success appeared to prove the viability of the FRAP formula of a narrow-front alliance or working-class bloc, the Communist Party leadership regarded FRAP as a mere steppingstone to a wider Popular Front alliance embracing one or both of the large non-Marxist left-of-center parties, that is, the Radicals and the Christian Democrats. Since a wide alliance of this type could have only limited aims and could not be based on a revolutionary platform, the Chilean Communists in 1959 appeared to be headed for a prolonged period of extreme moderation.

The Socialists, on the other hand, had no desire for a wider alliance, in which they would inevitably be relegated to a minor role and even run the risk of being isolated by a combination of the more flexible Communists and the non-Marxist partners of the alliance. Socialists and Communists were thus in fundamental disagreement as to the strategic aims of their alliance. A further cause of friction was the Socialists' enthusiasm for the economic doctrines of Titoism and for the Titoist foreign policy of nonalignment. To the Communists, Titoism had again[1] become a heresy that could not be tolerated within the ranks of the workers' movement. It may nevertheless be doubted that the Communist leaders would have emphasized this ideological difference of opinion quite so strongly if by the year 1959 they had not begun to regret their alliance with the Socialists, which had proved an obstacle to a broader alliance with non-Marxist parties.

At this point the psychological impact of the Cuban revolution completely changed the situation within the Chilean Left, giving the FRAP alliance a new meaning and a new lease on life.

It was not the Cuban doctrine of revolution by a combination of guerrilla warfare and urban terrorism that appealed to the Chilean Left. The leaders of the Communist and Socialist parties were not adventurers but experienced machine politicians; not for a moment did they contemplate the application of such methods in a country that has no guerrilla tradition and whose people have a highly developed sense of civic responsibility. What fascinated them were the developments after Castro's advent to power: the rapid socialization of the Cuban economy, Cuban defiance of the United States, and the political, military, and economic support of the revolutionary regime by the Soviet Union.

These events appeared to prove that confiscation of American property and the most radical forms of social revolution had now become possible in Latin America because the Soviet Union was both willing and able to

[1] Since the November 1957 meeting of communist parties in Moscow.

afford protection to Latin American revolutionary regimes. The Bay of Pigs disaster seemed to confirm that the United States was no longer strong enough to maintain its positions in the area; although desperately anxious to liquidate the Cuban regime, the United States government had apparently been too much afraid of Soviet reprisals to risk open military intervention and had had to resort to indirect intervention with totally inadequate means.

New perspectives were thus opened to the Latin American Left. Revolution was no longer a dream or a distant objective to be approached with circumspection. A Marxist regime had been established in a Latin American country at a distance of only ninety miles from the United States. It had confiscated all American property, socialized industry, and implemented a sweeping agrarian reform. This made it psychologically impossible for the Marxist parties of Chile, a country far less exposed to American armed intervention than Cuba, to aim for less. The FRAP alliance thereby acquired a revolutionary significance that it had hitherto lacked. This meant that the Chilean Communists had to give up their hopes of broadening the alliance by the inclusion of moderate democratic parties. Counter to their entire tradition and deep-rooted inclination, they had to accept the Socialist formula of a narrow, proletarian alliance confined to the workers' parties and a handful of unimportant "bourgeois" fellow travelers.

The revolutionary euphoria of the Left reached its height in 1962. Then came the Cuban missile crisis.

The missile crisis revealed that the United States was far stronger and the Soviet Union weaker than the Latin American leftists had assumed; that the Soviet

Union, and not the United States, would back down when faced with the prospect of nuclear war over a Latin American issue; that the American government had refrained from using its own military forces to invade Cuba not because it was afraid of Soviet reprisals but because it had not considered the Cuban threat to be serious enough to warrant such a measure; and that the United States was actually in a position to dictate what weapons the Soviets could maintain in their Caribbean base and what weapons they would have to withdraw. All this meant that Latin American revolutionary regimes during a real crisis would not be able to count on Soviet protection against United States intervention.

As the full significance of the missile crisis gradually became clear, a change of political mood and climate took place in Latin America. What had appeared to be a safe bet took on the aspect of a suicidal risk. Many of those who had intended to join the ranks of the revolutionaries in order to be on the winning side had second thoughts, while others who feared the revolution but had resigned themselves to its inevitability were now spurred to counteraction. Throughout 1963 the wave of communism and anti-American nationalism that had threatened to engulf Latin America receded; the frenzied efforts of the Venezuelan revolutionaries to turn the tide were unsuccessful.

One effect of the missile crisis was that disillusionment with the Soviet Union led many Latin American leftists to a reappraisal of the Sino-Soviet conflict. Before the missile crisis they had regarded this conflict as irrelevant to the Latin American situation, and Chinese criticism of Soviet foreign policy as unjustified.

The Chinese had accused the Soviet leaders of un-
revolutionary softness in their attitude toward the
"American imperialists," and even of planning to betray
the cause of world revolution by an arrangement with
the United States. This certainly did not seem to apply
to the Western Hemisphere, where the Soviet Union
was challenging the United States by its support of
Cuba. But after the missile crisis the Chinese accusations suddenly appeared more plausible.

In Chile the leaders of the Communist Party remained loyal to Moscow, and their authority was strong
enough to prevent the spread of pro-Chinese sympathies among the party members. Only an insignificant
number of Chilean Communists went over to the
Chinese camp. On the other hand, many Socialists and
the bulk of the non-Marxist fellow travelers of FRAP
openly took the Chinese side. But Red China is obviously not nearly strong enough to take over the role of
military protector of the Latin American revolution that
the Soviet Union could no longer be relied upon to play.
For this reason there is little prospect of the pro-Chinese
current in the Chilean Left developing into a vigorous
new trend; it is more a symptom of demoralization and
disintegration than anything else.

The leaders of the FRAP alliance failed to adjust their
policies to the new situation that had arisen as a result
of the missile crisis. The Socialists' stubborn refusal to
acknowledge the need for changes was understandable.
Their leader Ampuero was a Titoist who did not want
the Chilean revolution to follow the Cuban example of
complete alignment with the Soviet bloc. Even before
the missile crisis, at the height of the Chilean Left's
enthusiasm for Cuba and the Soviet Union, he had

insisted on an independent line.[2] He could thus hardly be expected to recognize that the Soviet and Cuban loss of prestige through the missile crisis called for a readjustment of FRAP policies. What he overlooked was that the enthusiasm of the FRAP propagandists for Cuba, presidential candidate Allende's repeated visits to Havana, and an election platform obviously inspired by the Cuban example had identified the FRAP cause so closely with that of Cuba and the Soviet Union that FRAP could not but be seriously affected by the missile crisis setback.

Their whole training and background rendered the Communist leaders far more sensitive to sudden changes of the international situation than the Socialists. The missile fiasco had not only halted Soviet penetration of Latin America; it had also eased the pressure on Berlin and caused the Soviet government to seek some degree of détente, however temporary, in its relations with the United States. This evidently called for a change of communist party policy in Latin America. Some of the Latin American communist parties succeeded in carrying out a change of front. In Peru the Communists and extreme nationalists had put up a joint candidate with a revolutionary platform in the presidential election of 1962, the results of which were voided by a military coup.[3] But when the military junta permitted a new presidential election in 1963, the Communists came out in support of the moderate Belaúnde Terry. In Argentina the Communists broke their alli-

[2] See Ampuero's 1962 debate with the Communists, Chapter 4, pp. 144–152.
[3] The motivation of the coup was the personal antagonism between one of the candidates, the moderate Haya de la Torre, and the military leaders, who favored another moderate, Belaúnde Terry.

ance with the militantly nationalist Peronistas and switched their allegiance to President Illía, also a moderate. It is significant that both Belaúnde Terry and Illía cooperated with the Alliance for Progress. Before the missile crisis, rejection of the Alliance for Progress had been the shibboleth by which the Communists determined whether a non-Communist politician was eligible for their support or was to be denounced as an agent of imperialism.

In Chile the obvious policy change for the Communists to undertake would have been reversion to their traditional policy of a broad alliance with limited aims. Specifically this would have meant swinging their support to the Christian Democrat Eduardo Frei. Unfortunately for the Communist leaders, the FRAP candidate Allende still seemed to have a fair chance of winning the election; there was not the remotest possibility of persuading the Socialists to withdraw him, and it was psychologically impossible for the Communists at this stage to break up the FRAP alliance and go over to Frei since the mass of their own supporters would have regarded this as rank treason. The Communists were thus forced to continue pursuit of a "narrow alliance" policy that was traditionally that of the Socialists and not their own. Although they were organizationally, financially, and numerically stronger than the Socialists, the Communists had become the prisoners of their weaker ally.

For a prolonged period the Communists at least held out against persistent Socialist demands to step up the propaganda campaign against Christian Democracy — a cautious attitude that clearly indicated their unhappiness with the "narrow alliance" policy and their hopes of someday, somehow, being able to revert to the "broad alliance" Popular Front strategy. But after the FRAP success in the Curicó by-election of March 1964[4] they gave up even this last remnant of an independent political concept and joined the Socialists in their furious anti-Christian-Democratic diatribes.

The surprise victory of Curicó misled the FRAP leaders, and even more their followers, into vastly overestimating their chances of success in the presidential election. Yet even in this state of elation their campaign tactics betrayed a fundamental lack of confidence in their cause. Their consistent refusal to debate the foreign policy implications of their electoral platform, that is, a conflict with the United States, was obviously due to the feeling that after the missile crisis this subject had become too painful to discuss. And whereas before the missile crisis FRAP propaganda had incessantly pointed to the Cuban example, it now avoided mention of Cuba and even neglected to defend the Cuban regime against its opponents' charges of tyranny and terrorism.

This election strategy was one of deception; it was an attempt to mislead part of the middle class, which by now was strongly anti-Cuban, into overlooking the obvious fact that FRAP's election program was inspired by the Cuban example.[5] The FRAP strategists assumed

---

[4] See Chapter 6, p. 208.

[5] Three weeks before the election, the Italian Communist tabloid *Paese Sera* belatedly published a year-old interview in which Allende had declared that Chile and all of Latin America would follow the Cuban example. The interview was of course widely publicized in Chile by the opponents of FRAP. Allende first denied having given the interview and then tried to explain his statement away. Some of his Socialist aides privately voiced the opinion that this was a case of deliberate Communist sabotage designed to lessen Allende's elec-

that the working-class vote was safe for Allende in any case — an assumption that was disproved by the election results.

An analysis of the election results shows the FRAP vote to have been strongest in the most backward sectors of the Chilean community, in the old, traditional Chile of superannuated copper and coal mines and inefficient, underequipped, and underproducing latifundia. In Chile the appeal of Marxism is evidently strongest wherever the economy is stagnant and the workingman has little or no prospect of advancement. But in the more dynamic urban Chile Frei won a majority even in the working-class districts.

The election results demonstrated the superiority of the typically Latin American formula of the "populist" party of broad appeal over the imported Marxist formula of the proletarian party. It was also a victory of the principles of democracy over those of Soviet and Cuban totalitarianism, and of a vigorous but rational common-sense nationalism over the extremes of irrational anti-American hysteria, a triumph of political realism over an adventurist doctrine that proclaimed

---

tion chances. A violently anticlerical speech by Communist Senator Jaime Barros, made at a time when the FRAP strategists were trying to build up a "Catholics for Allende" movement, was mentioned as another instance of deliberate sabotage. But Barros was an egregious aristocrat with a reputation for undisciplined behavior. His quarrel with the party leadership over the Catholic issue appears to have been genuine, since he later resigned from the party in disgust, giving this as his main reason. As for the untimely publication of the *Paese Sera* interview, this was probably nothing more than one of the unfortunate accidents that often bedevil even the most carefully planned election campaigns. My own impression was that from Curicó onward the Communists pulled their full weight in the campaign, and that their leaders were genuinely eager for an Allende victory, even though some of them may well have had qualms about the international complications that might arise from this event.

that salvation could be achieved through a conflict with the dominant power of the hemisphere.

But what if the missile crisis had not taken place or had ended in defeat for the United States instead of the Soviet Union? In that case the road advocated by the FRAP propagandists would no longer have appeared unrealistic and adventurous. Doubt and demoralization would have afflicted the democratic, not the Marxist, camp. Soviet strength would have appeared superior to that of the United States, and many opponents of communism would have been immobilized by the apparent inevitability of its triumph. The election results would then inevitably have been much more favorable to the Marxists — either victory or so close to victory as to enable them to sabotage the normal functioning of democracy and plunge Chile into a state of anarchy favorable to their designs.

We thus see that the fate of Chile was decisively influenced by an event in which that country was not directly involved: a confrontation between two great powers that took place on the other side of the continent, thousands of miles away. The missile crisis was not a planned result of American policy; the showdown was forced upon the United States government much against its will. Why then did the missile crisis stem the advance of communism in Chile and other Latin American countries so much more effectively than all the deliberate efforts undertaken by the United States in the course of a decade? The answer is that in the missile crisis the United States at long last departed from its established policy of attempting to contain communism and Soviet expansionism while avoiding a direct confrontation with the Soviet Union. This policy was doubtless motivated by a laudable reluctance to risk plunging the world into a nuclear war, but it had inevitably given the adversary an impression of fear and weakness, thus encouraging him to continue pursuit of his expansionist policy and constantly to increase its scope.

In Latin America the United States had first countered Soviet bloc arms shipments to Guatemala in 1954 by a CIA-sponsored coup against the procommunist government of that country. A similar move against Fidel Castro in 1961 met with spectacular failure, and so far neither the draconic economic sanctions against Cuba nor the encouragement of internal resistance and exile raids had achieved their aim. Meanwhile the United States government treated the man responsible for the arms shipments with circumspection bordering on deference, sitting in conference with him in Geneva, Camp David, and Vienna and even inviting him for a Grand Tour of the United States.

The policy of harassing the puny recipients of Soviet arms instead of facing up to the powerful supplier could hardly impress the Latin Americans as a sign of strength. Nor was it effective in avoiding a direct confrontation. It only postponed it, and when the showdown finally came in October 1962, it was on a far vaster scale and brought the world much closer to the brink of nuclear war than would have been the case if the United States government had notified Czechoslovakia in 1954, or the Soviet Union in 1960, that arms shipments to unfriendly Latin American countries would be intercepted. It might be argued that this would have been a violation of international law, but the breach of law would in any case have been less serious, and created a less unfavorable impression, than the coup against Arbenz or the Bay of Pigs adventure.

Another and far more positive and laudable move in the effort to halt the spread of communism in Latin America is the Alliance for Progress. The Alliance is of great value in winning the friendship of the moderate nationalist leaders who today are the most powerful and dynamic force in Latin America. But because it is so obviously a program set up to counteract Soviet and Cuban influence, many Latin Americans consider it to have an unpleasant flavor of bribery, which contributes to the general feeling that the United States is weak. This unfavorable impression can be dispelled only if the Alliance is supplemented by an energetic American foreign policy designed to persuade the Soviet Union that Latin America is out of its reach.

That cannot be achieved by action against the Soviet Union's Latin American collaborators. The Soviet Union will always find allies among Latin America's politicos, military men, and adventurers if it looks for them. After the removal of Arbenz it found Castro, and if Soviet expansion into the area had not been blocked by the missile crisis, Goulart of Brazil or Allende of Chile would have served the Soviet purpose quite as well or even more reliably. By themselves none of these men, nor any other Latin American political leader, can possibly threaten the security of the United States. They become dangerous only if and as long as they are backed by the Soviet Union.

The only real adversary of the United States in Latin America is the Soviet Union, and this adversary must be faced in direct confrontation. That is the lesson of the Cuban missile crisis. As long as the United States restricted itself to harassment of the Soviet Union's Latin American proxy Castro, the tide of communism and extreme nationalism in Latin America continued to rise. It began to recede as soon as a direct Soviet-American confrontation had dispelled the false impression of American weakness and Soviet superiority. The story of the Chilean Left from 1960 through 1964 is a particularly striking illustration of this general trend.

Appendix

THE ULTRALEFT

To the left of the Socialists and Communists there is a fringe territory populated by egregious individuals and tiny splinter groups that incessantly combine with and repel each other in the most varied combinations. Some of the groups may count less than a dozen members; the membership of the largest one, Vanguardia Revolucionaria Marxista, was variously estimated at from two to three hundred before it broke up into two rival movements in the spring of 1964.

There are two main trends among the Chilean ultraleft: a pro-Chinese one and a Trotskyist one. Neither of them has so far attained any importance, weight, or influence in Chilean political life, but in the aftermath of the FRAP coalition's defeat in the 1964 presidential election the pro-Chinese groups may become attractive to some disgruntled Communist Party cadres, and the Trotskyist groups to Socialists antagonized by Ampuero's methods of leadership.

PRO-CHINESE GROUPS

The main pro-Chinese organization is Spartacus, led by the seven Communist Party intellectuals who in March 1964 set up the publishing firm Espártaco Editores, that handles the distribution of Chinese propaganda materials in Chile and other Latin American countries.[1] Although one or two of them had some standing in Santiago leftist artistic and intellectual circles, none of them held any rank or position in the Communist Party. In October 1963 they were expelled from the party. They continued their work of distributing Chinese propaganda publications and in 1964 began to publish an ideological review, *Principios Marxista-Leninistas,* and a newssheet, *Combate,* which appear at infrequent intervals and are remarkable for their well-nigh incredibly low level of intellect and knowledge. Nevertheless the mere fact that Spartacus is the official representative of Chinese communism in Chile has given the group a certain prestige, so that it managed to win Salvador Allende and other top-ranking non-Communist representatives of the FRAP alliance as well as several prominent personalities of the Radical Party as sponsors of its 1964 Chinese revolution anniversary celebration. The Communist Party of Chile has so far been able to shield its membership against the full repercussions of the Sino-Soviet conflict. Once this is no longer possible, Spartacus may well become the nucleus of a larger pro-Chinese movement in the Chilean Left.

A second pro-Chinese group is composed of a faction of the ultraleftist organization Vanguardia Revolucion-

[1] See Chapter 5, pp. 223–224.

aria Marxista, which broke up early in 1964. It consists of the remnants of the Reinoso-Palma-Cares group that was expelled from the Communist Party in 1950.[2] In 1950 this dissident Communist group had fused with Enrique Sepúlveda's dissident Trotskyists to form Vanguardia; and in 1963 it had addressed a long open letter to the Central Committee of the Chinese Communist Party,[3] offering them its support and cooperation. The Chinese apparently demanded that Vanguardia get rid of its Trotskyist elements as a precondition to the establishment of relations, and this seems to have occasioned the 1964 split. The pro-Chinese faction of Vanguardia collaborates with Spartacus, and late in 1964 the two groups were negotiating a merger.

TROTSKYISTS AND SEMI-TROTSKYISTS

The main representative of this trend is a new grouping that calls itself the Partido Socialista Popular. This is the fusion of an old established Trotskyist grouping, Partido Obrero Revolucionario, with some small Socialist groups recently expelled from the Socialist Party in various provincial towns. The Partido Socialista Popular also counts two interesting independent personalities among its leaders. One of these is Clotario Blest, the Catholic ultraleftist and former president of the Trade Union Confederation, the story of whose conversion to Castroism has been told in Chapter 3. The other is Oscar Waiss, the Santiago lawyer who had been the Socialist Party's Secretary for International Relations and one of its leading ideologists. Waiss was

[2] See Chapter 3, p. 57.
[3] See *El Rebelde*, Vol. II, No. 18 (October 1963).

expelled from the party by Ampuero in 1961. He is the author of several books on socialist ideology and a brilliant, extraordinarily vituperative pamphleteer who may well be called the Thersites of the Chilean Left.

There are also some independent Trotskyist grouplets not affiliated with the Partido Socialista Popular. One of these is the Trotskyist faction of the Vanguardia Revolucionaria Marxista, and another the minute Partido Obrero Revolucionario (Trotskyists),[4] affiliated with a dissident, mainly Latin American faction of the Fourth International led by an Argentinian named J. Posadas.[5]

[4] Not to be confused with the already mentioned Partido Obrero Revolucionario that merged with the Partido Socialista Popular.

[5] This group publishes a newssheet devoted mainly to printing the voluminous but highly entertaining statements of Posadas, a man whose implacably logical train of thought is unchecked by any barrier of common sense. Thus Posadas is on record as having advocated nuclear warfare in support of world revolution: "The duty of the workers' states is to intervene with all their means and material forces, military, atomic, in support and encouragement of, and solidarity with, the world colonial revolution." (*Vanguardia Proletaria*, Vol. V, No. 36 [January 1963].) He also believes that socialist science could prevent earthquakes and hurricanes and thus comes to the logical conclusion that "these disasters are not a natural calamity but a result of social class relations that stem from the existence of capitalism." (*Ibid.*, Vol. V, No. 44 [October 1963].)

BIBLIOGRAPHY

BOOKS AND PAMPHLETS

Ahumada, Jorge. *En vez de la miseria.* 2nd ed. Santiago de Chile: Editorial Del Pacífico, S. A., 1958.

Alexander, Robert J. *Communism in Latin America.* 2nd printing. New Brunswick, N.J.: Rutgers University Press, 1960.

———. *Prophets of the Revolution: Profiles of Latin American Leaders.* New York: Macmillan, 1962.

———. *Today's Latin America.* New York: Doubleday, 1962.

Allende, Salvador. *Cuba, un camino.* Santiago de Chile: Prensa Latinoamericana, 1960.

Almeyda M., Clodomiro. *Reflexiones políticas.* Santiago de Chile: Prensa Latinoamericana, S. A., 1958.

———. *Visión sociológica de Chile.* Santiago de Chile: Academia de las Escuelas de Ciencias Políticas y Administrativas, 1957.

Boizard B., Ricardo. *Cuatro retratos en profundidad: Ibáñez, Lafertte, Leighton, Walker.* Santiago de Chile: Imprenta el Imparcial, 1950.

———. *La Democracia Cristiana en Chile (Un mundo que nace entre dos guerras).* Santiago de Chile: Editorial Orbe, 1963.

Calvez, Jean Ives, José Miguel Ibáñez, Roger Vekemans, Máximo

Pacheco, William Thayer, Jaime Castillo. *El marxismo, teoría y acción.* Santiago de Chile: Editorial Del Pacífico, S. A., 1964.

Cassigoli, Armando. *Discurso leído por el camarada Armando Cassigoli en el acto de homenage al décimoquarto aniversario de la revolución china.* Santiago de Chile, 1963. Mimeographed pamphlet.

Castillo Velasco, Jaime. *El problema comunista.* Santiago de Chile: Editorial Del Pacífico, S. A., 1955.

Castro, Josué de. *Geopolítica del hambre (ensayo sobre los problemas alimentarios y demográficos del mundo).* Buenos Aires: Ediciones Solar and Librería Hachette, S. A., 1962.

Congresos Internacionales Demócrata-Cristianos. Santiago de Chile: Editorial Del Pacífico, S. A., 1957.

Corporación de Fomento de la Producción. *Geografía económica de Chile.* 4 vols. Santiago de Chile, 1962.

Correa Prieto, Luis. *Nuestra economía y sus flaquezas: análisis no comprometido.* Santiago de Chile: Editorial Orbe, 1963.

———. *El Presidente Ibáñez: la política y los políticos.* Santiago de Chile: Editorial Orbe, 1962.

Corvalán Lépez, Luis. *Chile y el nuevo panorama mundial.* [Santiago de Chile]: Talleres Gráficos Lautaro, 1959.

———. *Nuestra vía revolucionaria.* 2nd ed. Santiago de Chile: Impresora Horizonte, 1964.

Cunill, Pedro. *Geografía de Chile.* Santiago de Chile: Editorial Universitaria, S. A., 1963.

Donoso, Ricardo. *Alessandri, agitador y demoledor.* México–Buenos Aires: Fondo de Cultura Económica, 1954.

Edwards Vives, Alberto. *La fronda aristocrática.* Santiago de Chile: Editorial Del Pacífico, S. A., 1959.

———, and Eduardo Frei. *Historia de los partidos políticos chilenos.* 2 vols. Santiago de Chile: Editorial Del Pacífico, S. A., 1949.

Encina, Francisco A. *Nuestra inferioridad económica: sus causas, sus consecuencias.* New ed. Santiago de Chile: Editorial Universitaria, S. A., 1955.

———, and Leopoldo Castedo. *Resumen de la historia de Chile.* 4th ed. Santiago de Chile: Empresa Editora Zig-Zag, S. A., 1961. Vols. II and III.

Frei, Eduardo. *Aún es tiempo.* Santiago de Chile: Talleres Gráficos el Chileno, 1942.

————. *Chile desconocido.* Santiago de Chile: Ediciones Ercilla, 1937.

————, and Ismael Bustos. *Maritain entre nosostros.* Santiago de Chile: Instituto de Educación Política, 1964.

————. *Pensamiento y acción.* Santiago de Chile: Editorial Del Pacífico, S. A., 1956.

Guerra Baeza, Hugo. *Portales y Rosas: contrapunto de hombres y políticas.* Santiago de Chile: Editorial Del Pacífico, S. A., 1958.

Guevara, Ernesto "Che." *Guerrilla Warfare.* New York: Monthly Review Press, 1961.

Guilisasti Tagle, Sergio. *Partidos políticos chilenos.* 2nd ed., enlarged. Santiago de Chile: Editorial Nascimento, 1964.

Hacia la conquista de un gobierno popular: documentos del XII Congreso Nacional del Partido Comunista de Chile. Santiago de Chile: Soc. Impresora "Horizonte," 1962.

Hurtado Cruchaga, Alberto, S.J. *El orden Social Cristiano en los documentos de la jerarquia católica.* Santiago de Chile: Club de Lectores, 1947.

————. *Sindicalismo (historia, teoría, práctica).* Santiago de Chile: Editorial Del Pacífico, S. A., 1950.

Jobet, Julio César. *Ensayo crítico del desarrollo económico-social de Chile.* Santiago de Chile: Editorial Universitaria, S. A., 1955.

————. *Los fundamentos del marxismo.* 4th ed. Santiago de Chile: Prensa Latinoamericana, 1964.

Ladrón de Guevara, Matilde. *Adiós al Cañaveral: diario de una mujer en Cuba.* 2nd ed. Buenos Aires: Editorial Goyanarte, 1962.

Lafertte, Elías. *Vida de un comunista (páginas autobiográficas).* Santiago de Chile: Talleres Gráficos Horizonte, 1961.

Lagas, Jacques. *Memorias de un capitán rebelde.* Santiago de Chile: Editorial Del Pacífico, S. A., 1964.

Lambert, Jacques. *Amérique Latine: Structures sociales et institutions politiques.* Paris: Presses Universitaires de France, 1963. (This penetrating study of the Latin American political system came to the author's attention too late to be cited in the text. It contains a detailed description of how Latin American parliamentary institutions are frequently used to block progress, and particularly to conserve a superannuated system of land tenure.)

Magnet, Alejandro. *Nuestros vecinos justicialistas*. Santiago de Chile: Editorial Del Pacífico, S. A., 1953.

———. *El Padre Hurtado*. Santiago de Chile: Editorial Del Pacífico, S. A., 1954.

Olavarría Bravo, Arturo. *Chile entre dos Alessandri: memorias políticas*. 2 vols. Santiago de Chile: Editorial Nascimento, 1962.

Oviedo, Benjamín. *La masoneria en Chile (bosquejo histórico)*. Santiago de Chile: Soc. Imp. y Lit. Universo, 1953.

Partido Comunista de Chile. *Documentos del XI Congreso Nacional realizado en noviembre de 1958*. Santiago de Chile: Talleres Gráficos Lautaro, 1959.

———. *El problema yugoslavo*. Santiago de Chile: Editora Austral, 1959.

El Partido Comunista de Chile y el movimiento comunista internacional: documentos e informes emanados de plenos y congresos del Partido Comunista de Chile. Santiago de Chile: Empresa Horizonte, [1964].

Pike, Frederick B. *Chile and the United States, 1880–1962*. Notre Dame: University of Notre Dame Press, 1963. (This book was unfortunately not available to the author during the time of writing and is therefore not cited in the text. It gives far more information than the title promises; it is both a history of modern Chile and a history of the major trends in Chilean political philosophy.)

Pinto Santa Cruz, Aníbal. *Chile, un caso de desarrollo frustrado*. 2nd ed. Santiago de Chile: Editorial Universitaria, S. A., 1962.

La polémica socialista-comunista. Published by the Central Committee of the Socialist Party. Santiago de Chile: Prensa Latinoamericana, S. A., [1962].

Poppino, Rollie E. *International Communism in Latin America: A History of the Movement, 1917–1963*. New York: Free Press of Glencoe, 1964.

Proposición acerca de la linea general del movimiento comunista internacional. Peking: Ediciones en Lenguas Extranjeras, 1963.

Ravines, Eudocio. *América Latina: un continente en erupción*. Buenos Aires: Editorial Claridad, S. A., 1956.

———. *La gran estafa*. 4th ed. Santiago de Chile: Editorial Del Pacífico, S. A., 1957.

Ricardo Fonseca: combatiente ejemplar. Prepared under the direction of the Secretariat of the Communist Party by the Commission of Historical Studies annexed to its Central Committee. Santiago de Chile: Talleres Gráficos Lautaro, 1952.

Silva Bascuñán, Alejandro. *Una experiencia Social Cristiana*. Santiago de Chile: Editorial Del Pacífico, S. A., 1949.

The South American Handbook, 1962. 38th ed. London: Trade and Travel Publications, 1962.

Sternberg, Marvin J. "Chilean Land Tenure and Land Reform." Ph.D. dissertation, University of California, 1962.

Stevenson, John Reese. *The Chilean Popular Front*. Philadelphia: University of Pennsylvania Press, 1942.

Treutler, Paul. *Andanzas de un alemán en Chile, 1851–1863*. Santiago de Chile: Editorial Del Pacífico, S. A., 1958.

Vergara, Marta. *Memorias de una mujer irreverente*. Santiago de Chile: Empresa Editora Zig-Zag, S. A., 1962.

Vitale, Luis. *Los discursos de Clotario Blest y la revolución chilena*. Santiago de Chile: Editorial POR, 1961.

———. *Esencia y apariencia de la Democracia Cristiana*. Santiago de Chile: Arancibia Hnos., 1964.

Waiss, Oscar. *Amanecer en Belgrado*. Santiago de Chile: Prensa Latinoamericana, S. A., 1956.

———. *Basura teórica y traición política*. Santiago de Chile: Ediciones "El Gallo Rojo," 1964.

———. *El espejismo del 64*. Santiago de Chile: Imprenta Victoria, 1962.

———. *Nacionalismo y socialismo en América Latina*. 2nd ed. Buenos Aires: Ediciones Iguazú, 1961.

———. *Socialismo sin gerentes*. Santiago de Chile, 1961.

Würth Rojas, Ernesto. *Ibáñez, caudillo enigmático*. Santiago de Chile: Editorial Del Pacífico, S. A., 1958.

JOURNALS, NEWSPAPERS, AND OTHER NEWSSHEETS

JOURNALS (all Santiago): *Arauco* (Socialist), *Aurora* (Communist), *Mensaje* (Catholic), *Nuestra Epoca* (Communist), *Polémica* (independent leftist Trotskyist), *Política y Espíritu* (Christian Democratic), *Principios* (Communist), *Principios Marxista-Leninistas* (pro-Chinese Communist), *Vistazo* (Communist illustrated weekly).

NEWSPAPERS (all Santiago): *Clarín* (independent leftist), *Diario Ilustrado* (Conservative), *El Mercurio* (independent), *Noticias de Última Hora* (independent, pro-Socialist), *El Siglo* (Communist).

NEWSSHEETS (intermittently issued; all Santiago): *Combate* (dissident Communist), *El Gallo Rojo* (MRC), *El Guerrillero Manuel Rodríguez, Vanguardia Proletaria* (Trotskyist), *El Rebelde* (Vanguardia Revolucionaria Marxista).

INDEX